STECK-VAUGHN

LEVEL

F

Language

EXERCISES

STECK-VAUGHN
C O M P A N Y

Acknowledgments

Senior Editor: Diane Sharpe
Project Editor: Stephanie Muller
Product Development: The Wheetley Company, Inc.
Cover Design: Sue Heatly Design

Macmillan Publishing Company: Pronunciation Key, reprinted with permission of the publisher, from *Macmillan School Dictionary 1.* Copyright © 1990 Macmillan Publishing Company, a division of Macmillan, Inc.

LANGUAGE EXERCISES Series:

Level A/Pink	Level D/Gray	Level G/Gold
Level B/Orange	Level E/Red	Level H/Green
Level C/Violet	Level F/Blue	Review/Yellow

ISBN 0-8114-4195-4

7 8 9 10 PO 00 99 98 97 96 95 94

Table of Contents

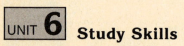

UNIT 5 Composition

UNIT 6 Study Skills

Final Reviews

Synonyms and Antonyms

■ A **synonym** is a word that has the same or nearly the same meaning as one or more other words.   EXAMPLE: joy – happiness

A. Write a synonym for each word below.

1. small _____
2. swiftly _____
3. weary _____
4. pretty _____
5. large _____
6. awful _____
7. lad _____
8. forest _____
9. cry _____
10. leap _____

11. wealthy _____
12. ugly _____
13. enough _____
14. begin _____
15. separate _____
16. exhausted _____
17. stare _____
18. rude _____
19. error _____
20. dirt _____

21. autumn _____
22. hurry _____
23. funny _____
24. build _____
25. discover _____
26. sick _____
27. seize _____
28. select _____
29. close _____
30. all _____

■ An **antonym** is a word that has the opposite meaning of another word.   EXAMPLE: hot – cold

B. Write an antonym for each word below.

1. good _____
2. old _____
3. dull _____
4. thick _____
5. tall _____
6. crooked _____
7. happy _____
8. remember _____
9. ugly _____
10. near _____

11. obey _____
12. rich _____
13. thin _____
14. narrow _____
15. useful _____
16. strong _____
17. lost _____
18. yes _____
19. careless _____
20. success _____

21. graceful _____
22. quiet _____
23. arrive _____
24. late _____
25. kind _____
26. empty _____
27. heavy _____
28. frown _____
29. rough _____
30. go _____

Homonyms

> ■ A **homonym** is a word that sounds the same as another word but has a different spelling and a different meaning.
>
> EXAMPLES: to – two – too   sum – some

A. Write a homonym for each word below.

1. hall _____	11. flower _____	21. our _____
2. threw _____	12. stair _____	22. sea _____
3. weak _____	13. pale _____	23. right _____
4. there _____	14. ring _____	24. peace _____
5. heard _____	15. soar _____	25. no _____
6. here _____	16. calc _____	26. grate _____
7. by _____	17. won _____	27. way _____
8. pane _____	18. aisle _____	28. cent _____
9. heal _____	19. rode _____	29. dew _____
10. blew _____	20. meet _____	30. forth _____

B. Underline the correct homonym(s) in each sentence below.

1. The couple walked for a mile along the (beech, beach).

2. Are there any (dear, deer) in these hills?

3. How much do you (way, weigh)?

4. Who broke this window (pane, pain)?

5. I have (to, too, two) go (to, too, two) the sale with those (to, too, two) people.

6. Laurie (knew, new) how to play a (new, knew) word game.

7. Juan and Luis spent a week at (there, their) grandparents' ranch.

8. Those boys (ate, eight) (ate, eight) of the apples we had just bought.

9. I like to walk by the (see, sea) at dusk.

10. (Wring, Ring) the bell, Matt.

11. Did you see what she brought (hear, here)?

12. He cannot (write, right) with his (write, right) hand.

13. Who has not (read, red) the magazine?

14. He found it cheaper to (buy, by) his pencils (buy, by) the box.

15. Chris told his niece a fairy (tale, tail).

> ■ A **homograph** is a word that has the same spelling as another word but a different meaning and sometimes a different pronunciation.
>
> EXAMPLE: <u>bow</u>, meaning "to bend the upper part of the body forward in respect," and <u>bow</u>, meaning "a weapon for shooting arrows"

■ **Circle the letter of the correct definition for each underlined homograph. Then write a sentence using the other meaning of the homograph.**

1. Put your pennies in the coin <u>bank</u>.

   a. a place where people save money   **b.** the ground along a river

   _____

2. If you <u>hide</u> your bank, be sure to remember where you put it.

   a. keep out of sight   **b.** the skin of an animal

   _____

3. Some people keep their money in a <u>safe</u>.

   a. a metal box with a lock   **b.** free from danger

   _____

4. There are only two people who have the <u>key</u> to open the safe.

   a. a piece of metal to open a lock   **b.** a low island or reef

   _____

5. Many people have an <u>account</u> at a bank.

   a. explanation   **b.** an amount of money

   _____

6. The bank downtown has a large steel <u>vault</u> for keeping valuables.

   a. leap or jump over using a pole   **b.** a safe room for storage

   _____

7. People who have bank accounts can pay for things by writing <u>checks</u>.

   a. pieces of paper that transfer money   **b.** a pattern of small squares

   _____

8. Some bank accounts earn <u>interest</u>.

   a. a feeling of curiosity   **b.** an amount of money

   _____

9. The guards in the bank watch the customers on television <u>screens</u>.

   a. a surface on which a picture is formed   **b.** wire over a window

   _____

Prefixes

> - A **prefix** added to the beginning of a base word changes the meaning of the word.
>   - EXAMPLE: un-, meaning "not," + the base word <u>done</u> = <u>undone</u>, meaning "not done"
> - Some prefixes have one meaning, and others have more than one meaning.
>   - EXAMPLES:
>
> | prefix | meaning |
> |---|---|
> | im-, in-, non-, un- | not |
> | dis-, in-, non- | opposite of, lack of, not |
> | mis- | bad, badly, wrong, wrongly |
> | pre- | before |
> | re- | again |

A. Add the prefix un-, im-, non-, or mis- to the base word in parentheses. Write the new word in the sentence. Then write the definition of the new word on the line after the sentence. Use a dictionary if necessary.

1. It is _____ (practical) to put a new monkey into a cage with other monkeys.

   _____

2. The monkeys might _____ (behave) with a newcomer among them.

   _____

3. They will also feel quite _____ (easy) for a number of days or even weeks.

   _____

4. Even if the new monkey is _____ (violent) in nature, the others may harm it.

   _____

5. Sometimes animal behavior can be quite _____ (usual).

   _____

B. Underline each prefix. Write the meaning of each word that has a prefix.

1. unexpected guest _____

2. really disappear _____

3. disagree often _____

4. misspell a name _____

5. preview a movie _____

6. reenter a room _____

7. misplace a shoe _____

8. impossible situation _____

9. nonstop reading _____

10. unimportant discussion _____

11. insane story _____

12. prejudge a person _____

- A **suffix** added to the end of a base word changes the meaning of the word.
  EXAMPLE: -ful, meaning "full of," + the base word <u>joy</u> = <u>joyful</u>, meaning "full of joy"
- Some suffixes have one meaning, and others have more than one meaning.
  EXAMPLES:

suffix	meaning
-able	able to be, suitable or inclined to
-al	relating to, like
-ful	as much as will fill, full of
-less	without, that does not
-ous	full of
-y	having, full of

A. Add a suffix from the list above to the base word in parentheses. Write the new word. Then write the definition of the new word on the line after the sentence. Do not use any suffix more than once.

1. Switzerland is a _____ country. (mountain)

_____

2. If you visit there, it is _____ to have a walking stick.   (help)

_____

3. Many tourists visit the country's _____ mountains to ski each year. (snow)

_____

4. The Swiss people have a great deal of _____ pride. (nation)

_____

5. Many Swiss are _____ about several languages. (knowledge)

_____

B. Underline each suffix. Write the meaning of each word that has a suffix.

1. breakable toy _____

2. endless waves _____

3. hazardous path _____

4. inflatable raft _____

5. poisonous snake _____

6. dependable trains _____

7. humorous program _____

8. tearful goodbye _____

9. bumpy ride _____

10. careless driver _____

11. natural food _____

12. magical wand _____

Contractions

> - A **contraction** is a word formed by joining two other words.
> - An **apostrophe** shows where a letter or letters have been left out.   EXAMPLE: do not = don't
> - <u>Won't</u> is an exception.   EXAMPLE: will not = won't

A. Underline each contraction. Write the words that make up each contraction on the line.

1. Stringrays look as if they're part bird, part fish. _____

2. Stingrays cover themselves with sand so they won't be seen. _____

3. There's a chance that waders might step on a stingray and get stung. _____

4. That's a painful way to learn that you shouldn't forget about stingrays.

   _____   _____

5. Until recently, stingrays weren't seen very often. _____

6. It doesn't seem likely, but some stingrays will eat out of divers' hands. _____

7. Because its mouth is underneath, the stingray can't see what it's eating.

   _____   _____

8. Once they've been fed by hand, they'll flutter around for more.

   _____   _____

9. It's hard to believe these stingrays aren't afraid of humans.

   _____   _____

10. To pet a stingray, they'd gently touch its velvety skin. _____

B. Find the pairs of words that can be made into contractions. Underline each pair. Then write the contraction each word pair can make on the lines following the sentences.

1. I have never tried scuba diving, but I would like to.

   _____   _____

2. It is a good way to explore what is under the water.

   _____   _____

3. First, I will need to take lessons in the pool. _____

4. Then I can find out what to do if the equipment does not work. _____

Compound Words

7

> - A **compound word** is a word that is made up of two or more words. The meaning of a compound word is related to the meaning of each individual word.
>   EXAMPLE: sun + glasses = sunglasses, meaning "glasses to wear in the sun"
> - Compound words may be written as one word, as hyphenated words, or as two separate words.
>   EXAMPLES: highway   high-rise   high school

A. Answer the following questions.

1. Something that has sharp, curved points extending backward is said to be barbed.

   What is barbed wire? _____

2. Dry means "without water." What does dry-clean mean? _____

3. Head means "a heading." What is a headline? _____

4. A deputy is "a person appointed to take the place of another."

   What is a deputy marshal? _____

5. Bare means "without a covering." What does bareback mean? _____

6. A road is a route. What is a railroad? _____

7. A paper is a type of document. What is a newspaper? _____

8. Blue is a color. What is a blueberry? _____

B. Combine words from the box to make compound words. Use the compound words to complete the sentences. You will use one word twice.

cut	every	fore	hair	head	where
loud	news	speaker	stand	thing	

1. Bob's hair covered his _____.

2. He knew it was time to get a _____.

3. He saw a truck hit a fire hydrant, which sprayed water _____.

4. The corner _____ was soaked.

5. A police officer used a _____ to direct traffic.

6. It was so exciting, Bob forgot about _____, including his haircut!

Connotation/Denotation

> - The **denotation** of a word is its exact meaning as stated in a dictionary.
>   EXAMPLE: The denotation of skinny is "very thin."
> - The **connotation** of a word is an added meaning that suggests something positive or negative.
>   EXAMPLES: **Negative:** Skinny suggests "too thin." Skinny has a negative connotation.
>   **Positive:** Slender suggests "attractively thin." Slender has a positive connotation.
> - Some words are neutral. They do not suggest either good or bad feelings.
>   EXAMPLES: month, building, chair

A. Underline the word in parentheses that has the more positive connotation.

1. Our trip to the amusement park was (fine, wonderful).

2. (Brave, Foolhardy) people rode on the roller coaster.

3. We saw (fascinating, weird) animals in the animal house.

4. Some of the monkeys made (hilarious, amusing) faces.

5. Everyone had a (smile, smirk) on his or her face on the way home.

B. Underline the word in parentheses that has the more negative connotation.

1. We bought (cheap, inexpensive) souvenirs at the amusement park.

2. I ate a (soggy, moist) sandwich.

3. Mike (nagged, reminded) us to go to the funny house.

4. The funny house was (comical, silly).

5. I didn't like the (smirk, grin) on the jester's face.

6. It made me feel (uneasy, frightened).

C. Answer the following questions.

1. Which is worth more, something old or something antique? _____

2. Is it better to be slender or to be skinny? _____

3. Which would you rather be called, thrifty or cheap? _____

4. Would a vain person be more likely to stroll or to parade? _____

5. Which is more serious, a problem or a disaster? _____

6. Is it more polite to sip a drink or to gulp it? _____

7. If you hadn't eaten for weeks, would you be hungry or starving? _____

8. After walking in mud, would your shoes be dirty or filthy? _____

Idioms

> ■ An **idiom** is an expression that has a meaning different from the usual meanings of the individual words within it.
> EXAMPLE: To lend a hand means "to help," not "to loan someone a hand."

A. Match the idioms underlined in the sentences below with their meanings. Write the correct letter on each line.

a. in a risky situation

b. do less than I should

c. admit having said the wrong thing

d. play music after only hearing it

e. spend money carefully

f. continue to have hope

g. listen with all your attention

h. teasing

i. accept defeat

j. meet by chance

_____ 1. I had hoped to run across some old friends at the ball game.

_____ 2. Their team was ready to throw in the towel when we scored our tenth run!

_____ 3. Peggy was pulling my leg when she told me that there are koala bears in Africa.

_____ 4. I told her that she was skating on thin ice when she tried to trick me.

_____ 5. My big sister must make ends meet with the little money she has for college.

_____ 6. Our parents told her, "Always keep your chin up when things get difficult."

_____ 7. José can play by ear the theme songs to all his favorite movies.

_____ 8. If you don't believe me, just be all ears when he plays.

_____ 9. My brother said that I would lie down on the job if he weren't watching over me.

_____ 10. I told Bill that he would eat his words once he saw how much work I had done.

B. Underline the idioms in the following sentences. On the line after each sentence, explain what the idiom means. Use a dictionary if necessary.

1. My parents and I don't always see eye to eye on what is meant by "clean."

_____

2. They think it means to take the bull by the horns and put everything away.

_____

3. It really gets their goat when I don't clean under my bed.

_____

4. From now on, I'm turning over a new leaf and doing a thorough job.

_____

5. Never again will my parents hit the ceiling when they see my room.

_____

A. Write a synonym and an antonym for each underlined word below.

1. a <u>pleasant</u> trip _____ _____

2. to <u>increase</u> speed _____ _____

3. an <u>awful</u> mistake _____ _____

4. a <u>funny</u> joke _____ _____

B. Underline the correct homonyms in each sentence below.

1. If you go by (plane, plain), you'll arrive (there, their) quicker than by bus.

2. A bus could take a (weak, week), but you'll get (to, too, two) (see, sea) more.

3. If you couldn't (bear, bare) a long trip, an overnight trip (wood, would) do instead.

C. Circle the letter of the correct definition for each underlined homograph. Then write a sentence using the other meaning of the homograph.

1. If you like to feel the <u>wind</u> in your hair, you might like sailing.

    a. moving air   **b.** to wrap in a circle

    _____

2. A sailboat will often <u>heel</u> if the sails are tight and the winds are strong.

    a. the rounded back part of the foot   **b.** lean to one side

    _____

D. Underline the prefix or suffix in each phrase below. Then write the meaning of each word that has the prefix or suffix.

1. impossible problem _____

2. dusty trails _____

3. hazardous road _____

4. incomplete work _____

5. uneasy feeling _____

6. nonviolent protest _____

7. helpless kitten _____

8. beautiful scene _____

E. Underline the idiom in each of the following sentences. On the line after the sentence, explain what the idiom means.

1. Stay on your toes while riding a bicycle. _____

2. If you run across a friend, pull over to the curb to talk. _____

F. Underline the word with a positive connotation in each pair of phrases below.

1. **a.** cheap material   **b.** inexpensive material

2. **a.** a cozy apartment   **b.** a cramped apartment

A. Rewrite the following sentences, using synonyms for the underlined words.

1. The lightning flashed across the black sky as the trees bent in the wind.

   _____

2. Blasts of wind whistled through the openings between the boards on the window.

   _____

3. Then a hush seemed to fall over our part of the world.

   _____

B. Rewrite the following sentences, using antonyms for the underlined words.

1. Before the storm hit, the sky got darker.

   _____

2. Black clouds drifted across the evening sky.

   _____

3. The heavy wind was blowing leaves over the trees.

   _____

C. Write a sentence using a homonym for each underlined word.

1. new _____

2. grater _____

3. choose _____

4. weight _____

5. waist _____

D. For each homograph below, write two sentences. Be sure to use a different meaning of the homograph in each sentence.

1. light a. _____

   b. _____

2. shed a. _____

   b. _____

3. rest a. _____

   b. _____

E. Add one of the following prefixes or suffixes to each base word to make a new word.

> **Prefixes:** in-, non-, dis-, mis-, pre-, re-
> **Suffixes:** -able, -ful, -less

1. place _____
2. direct _____
3. use _____
4. measure _____
5. speech _____

6. tire _____
7. remark _____
8. spell _____
9. pay _____
10. fund _____

F. Use the following idioms in sentences. Use a dictionary if necessary.

1. throw in the towel _____
2. pulling my leg _____
3. skating on thin ice _____
4. get in touch with _____
5. keep an eye on _____

G. Think of words that have almost the same meaning as the neutral word, but have a more negative or positive connotation. Complete the chart with your words.

Negative Connotation	Neutral	Positive Connotation
1. _____	wet	_____
2. _____	shout	_____
3. _____	thin	_____
4. _____	old	_____
5. _____	talk	_____
6. _____	clothes	_____
7. _____	ask	_____
8. _____	work	_____
9. _____	cut	_____
10. _____	eat	_____

Recognizing Sentences

> ■ A **sentence** is a group of words that expresses a complete thought.
> EXAMPLE: Marie sings well.

■ Some of the following groups of words are sentences, and some are not. Write <u>S</u> before each group that is a sentence. Punctuate each sentence with a period.

_____ 1. When the downhill skiing season begins____

_____ 2. Last summer I visited my grandparents in New Jersey____

_____ 3. From the very beginning of the first-aid lessons____

_____ 4. One of the little girls from the neighborhood____

_____ 5. A visiting musician played the organ____

_____ 6. On the way to school this morning____

_____ 7. "I love you, Mother," said little Mike____

_____ 8. The blue house at the corner of Maple Street____

_____ 9. After Emily left, the phone rang off the hook____

_____ 10. Speak distinctly and loudly so that you can be heard____

_____ 11. I have finally learned to drive our car____

_____ 12. This is William's tenth birthday____

_____ 13. At the very last moment, we were ready____

_____ 14. When you speak in front of people____

_____ 15. The basket of fruit on the table____

_____ 16. Please answer the telephone, Julia____

_____ 17. Hurrying to class because he is late____

_____ 18. The first thing in the morning____

_____ 19. That mistake was costly and unfortunate____

_____ 20. We are planning to make a new doghouse____

_____ 21. The dog chased the cat up the tree____

_____ 22. Daniel Boone was born in Pennsylvania____

_____ 23. The giant cottonwood in our backyard____

_____ 24. Marla, bring my notebook____

_____ 25. On a stool beside the back door____

_____ 26. Sometimes the noise from the street____

_____ 27. Somewhere out of state____

_____ 28. The band played a lively march____

_____ 29. That flight arrived on time____

_____ 30. Was cracked in dozens of places____

> - A **declarative** sentence makes a statement. It is followed by a period (.).   EXAMPLES: It is warm today. I took off my coat.
> - An **interrogative** sentence asks a question. It is followed by a question mark (?).   EXAMPLES: When is Tony coming? Why is the bus late today?

■ **Write D before each declarative sentence and IN before each interrogative sentence. Put the correct punctuation mark at the end of the sentence.**

_____IN_____ 1. Who is your favorite author _?_

_____ 2. How are our forests protected from fire____

_____ 3. Tim learned the names of the trees in his neighborhood____

_____ 4. A good driver obeys every traffic law____

_____ 5. The hippopotamus lives in Africa____

_____ 6. Do you know the legend of the dogwood tree____

_____ 7. Every sentence should begin with a capital letter____

_____ 8. Ryan is repairing the lamp____

_____ 9. Did you ever see a kangaroo____

_____ 10. Where did these fragrant roses grow____

_____ 11. Beautiful furniture can be made from the oak tree____

_____ 12. Flour can be made from dried bananas____

_____ 13. Did anyone find Steve's book____

_____ 14. Andrea feeds the goldfish every day____

_____ 15. How many people are studying to be pilots____

_____ 16. Kelly is going to the show with us____

_____ 17. Last summer we made a trip to Carlsbad Caverns____

_____ 18. How old are you____

_____ 19. The architect and her assistant inspected the building____

_____ 20. When did you arrive at the meeting____

_____ 21. Did you forget your wallet____

_____ 22. That light bulb is burned out____

_____ 23. The baby crawled across the room____

_____ 24. When would you like to eat____

_____ 25. Jo helped Andy wash the car____

_____ 26. Did they wax the car____

_____ 27. How did you make that sand castle____

_____ 28. It is easy to make if we work together____

- An **imperative** sentence expresses a command or a request. It is followed by a period (.). EXAMPLE: Close the door.
- An **exclamatory** sentence expresses strong or sudden feeling. It is followed by an exclamation point (!). EXAMPLE: I am innocent!

- Write **IM** before each imperative sentence and **E** before each exclamatory sentence. Put the correct punctuation mark at the end of each sentence.

IM	**1.**	Write the names of the days of the week___ .
_____	**2.**	Please mail this package for me___
_____	**3.**	I love the gift you gave me___
_____	**4.**	Lay the papers on the desk___
_____	**5.**	How beautiful the night is___
_____	**6.**	Watch out for that turning car___
_____	**7.**	Drive more slowly___
_____	**8.**	Keep time with the music___
_____	**9.**	Deliver this message immediately___
_____	**10.**	Sign your name in my yearbook___
_____	**11.**	That airplane is so huge___
_____	**12.**	Please lend me a postage stamp___
_____	**13.**	I'm delighted with the flowers___
_____	**14.**	How blue the sky is___
_____	**15.**	My neighbor's shed is on fire___
_____	**16.**	The baby's lip is bleeding___
_____	**17.**	I can't believe that I got a perfect score___
_____	**18.**	Pass the green beans___
_____	**19.**	Write down these sentences___
_____	**20.**	That movie was so exciting___
_____	**21.**	The puppy is so playful___
_____	**22.**	Look both ways when crossing the street___
_____	**23.**	What a pretty red and blue sailboat___
_____	**24.**	Please repeat what you said___
_____	**25.**	Put the vase on the table___
_____	**26.**	Be more careful with your work___
_____	**27.**	That's a fantastic book to read___
_____	**28.**	This is a wonderful surprise___

> - Every sentence has two main parts, a **complete subject** and a **complete predicate.**
> - The complete subject includes all the words that tell who or what the sentence is about.
>   EXAMPLES: **My brother**/likes to go with us. **Six geese**/honked loudly.
> - The complete predicate includes all the words that state the action or condition of the subject.
>   EXAMPLES: My brother/**likes to go with us.** Six geese/**honked loudly.**

■ **Draw a line between the complete subject and the complete predicate in each sentence.**

1. Bees/fly.

2. Trains whistle.

3. A talented artist drew this cartoon.

4. The wind blew furiously.

5. My grandmother made this dress last year.

6. We surely have enjoyed the holiday.

7. These cookies are made with rice.

8. This letter came to the post office box.

9. They rent a cabin in Colorado every summer.

10. Jennifer is reading about the pioneer days in the West.

11. Our baseball team won the third game of the series.

12. The band played a cheerful tune.

13. A cloudless sky is a great help to a pilot.

14. The voice of the auctioneer was heard throughout the hall.

15. A sudden flash of lightning startled us.

16. The wind howled down the chimney.

17. Paul's dog followed him to the grocery store.

18. Their apartment is on the sixth floor.

19. We have studied many interesting places.

20. Each player on the team deserves credit for the victory.

21. Forest rangers fought the raging fire.

22. A little spider taught Robert a valuable lesson.

23. Millions of stars make up the Milky Way.

24. The airplane was lost in the thick clouds.

25. Many of the children waded in the pool.

26. Yellowstone Park is the largest of our national parks.

27. Cold weather is predicted for tomorrow.

28. The trees were covered with moss.

> - The **simple subject** of a sentence is the main word in the complete subject. The simple subject is a noun or a word that stands for a noun.
>   EXAMPLE: My **sister**/lost her gloves.
> - Sometimes the simple subject is also the complete subject.
>   EXAMPLE: **She**/lost her gloves.
> - The **simple predicate** of a sentence is a verb within the complete predicate. The simple predicate may be a one-word verb or a verb of more than one word.
>   EXAMPLES: She/**lost** her gloves. She/**is looking** for them.

- **Draw a line between the complete subject and complete predicate in each sentence below. Underline the simple subject once and the simple predicate twice.**

1. A sudden <u>clap</u> of thunder/<u>frightened</u> all of us.
2. The soft snow covered the fields and roads.
3. We drove very slowly over the narrow bridge.
4. The students are making an aquarium.
5. Our class read about the founder of Hull House.
6. The little girls were playing in the park.
7. This album has many folk songs.
8. We are furnishing the sandwiches for tonight's picnic.
9. All the trees on that lawn are giant oaks.
10. Many Americans are working in foreign countries.
11. The manager read the names of the contest winners.
12. Bill brought these large melons.
13. We opened the front door of the house.
14. The two mechanics worked on the car for an hour.
15. Black and yellow butterflies fluttered among the flowers.
16. The little girl spoke politely.
17. We found many beautiful shells along the shore.
18. The best part of the program is the dance number.
19. Every ambitious person is working hard.
20. Sheryl swam across the lake two times.
21. Our program will begin promptly at eight o'clock.
22. The handle of this basket is broken.
23. The clock in the tower strikes every hour.
24. The white farmhouse on that road belongs to my cousin.
25. The first game of the season will be played tomorrow.

Subjects and Predicates in Inverted Order

15

- When the subject of a sentence comes before all or part of the predicate, the sentence is in **natural order.**
  - EXAMPLE: The puppy scampered away.
- When all or part of the predicate comes before the subject, the sentence is in **inverted order.**
  - EXAMPLE: Away scampered the puppy.
- Many interrogative sentences are in inverted order.
  - EXAMPLE: Where is/James?

A. Draw a line between the complete subject and the complete predicate in each sentence. Write <u>I</u> in front of sentences that are in inverted order.

_____I_____   **1.** Lightly falls/the mist.

_____   **2.** The peaches on this tree are ripe now.

_____   **3.** Over and over rolled the rocks.

_____   **4.** Down the street marched the band.

_____   **5.** Near the ocean are many birds.

_____   **6.** Right under the chair ran the kitten.

_____   **7.** He hit the ball a long way.

_____   **8.** Along the ridge hiked the campers.

_____   **9.** Underground is the stream.

_____   **10.** The fish jumped in the lake.

_____   **11.** Over the hill came the trucks.

_____   **12.** Out came the rainbow.

B. Rewrite each inverted sentence in Exercise A in natural order.

1. _____

2. _____

3. _____

4. _____

5. _____

6. _____

7. _____

8. _____

9. _____

Using Compound Subjects

> ■ Two sentences in which the subjects are different but the predicates are the same can be combined into one sentence. The two subjects are joined by <u>and</u>. The subject of the new sentence is called a **compound subject.**
> EXAMPLE: **Lynn** visited an amusement park.
> **Eric** visited an amusement park.
> **Lynn and Eric** visited an amusement park.

A. Draw a line between the complete subject and the complete predicate in each sentence. If the subject is compound, write <u>CS</u> before the sentence.

 __CS__ 1. English settlers and Spanish settlers/came to North America in the 1600s.

_____ 2. Trees and bushes were chopped down to make room for their houses.

_____ 3. The fierce winds and the cold temperatures made the first winters very harsh.

_____ 4. The settlers and Native Americans became friends.

_____ 5. Native Americans helped the settlers grow food in the new country.

_____ 6. Potatoes and corn were first grown by Native Americans.

_____ 7. English settlers and Spanish settlers had never tasted turkey.

_____ 8. Peanuts and sunflower seeds are Native American foods that we now eat for snacks.

_____ 9. Lima beans and corn are combined to make succotash.

_____ 10. Zucchini is an American squash that was renamed by Italian settlers.

_____ 11. Native Americans also introduced barbecuing to the settlers.

B. Combine each pair of sentences below. Underline the compound subject.

1. Gold from the New World was sent to Spain. Silver from the New World was sent to Spain.

_____

_____

2. France staked claims in the Americas in the 1500s and 1600s. The Netherlands staked claims in the Americas in the 1500s and 1600s.

_____

_____

3. John Cabot explored areas of the Americas. Henry Hudson explored areas of the Americas.

_____

_____

C. Write a sentence with a compound subject.

_____

_____

Using Compound Predicates

> ■ Two sentences in which the subjects are the same but the predicates are different can be combined into one sentence. The two predicates may be joined by or, and, or but. The predicate of the new sentence is called a **compound predicate.**
>
> EXAMPLE: The crowd **cheered** the players.
> The crowd **applauded** the players.
> The crowd **cheered and applauded** the players.

A. Draw a line between the complete subject and the complete predicate in each sentence. If the predicate is compound, write CP before the sentence.

_____ 1. The students organized a picnic for their families.

_____ 2. They discussed and chose a date for the picnic.

_____ 3. They wrote and designed invitations.

_____ 4. The invitations were mailed and delivered promptly.

_____ 5. Twenty-five families responded to the invitations.

_____ 6. The students bought the food and made the sandwiches.

_____ 7. The families bought the soft drinks.

_____ 8. The students packed and loaded the food into a truck.

_____ 9. The families brought and set up the volleyball nets.

_____ 10. Everyone participated in the games and races.

_____ 11. They ran relay races and threw water balloons.

_____ 12. Everyone packed the food and cleaned up the picnic area at the end of the day.

B. Combine each pair of sentences below. Underline the compound predicate.

1. Caroline heard the music. Caroline memorized the music.

_____

_____

2. Keith picked up the newspapers. Keith loaded the newspapers onto his bike.

_____

_____

3. Larry studied the names of the states. Larry wrote down the names of the states.

_____

_____

C. Write a sentence with a compound predicate.

_____

Simple and Compound Sentences

18

- A **simple sentence** has one subject and one predicate.
  EXAMPLE: The earth/is covered by land and water.
- A **compound sentence** is made up of two simple sentences joined by a connecting word such as <u>and</u>, <u>but</u>, and <u>or</u>. A comma is placed before the connecting word.
  EXAMPLE: One-fourth of the earth/is covered by land, and the land/is divided into seven continents.

A. Draw a line between the complete subject and the complete predicate in each sentence. Write <u>S</u> before each simple sentence. Write <u>C</u> before each compound sentence.

_____ **1.** The seven continents of the world are North America, South America, Africa, Europe, Australia, Asia, and Antarctica.

_____ **2.** Three-fourths of the earth is covered by water, and most of it is salty ocean water.

_____ **3.** The four oceans of the world are the Pacific, the Atlantic, the Indian, and the Arctic.

_____ **4.** We cannot exist without water, but we cannot drink the salty ocean water.

_____ **5.** Most of the water we drink comes from lakes, rivers, and streams.

_____ **6.** Clean water is a priceless resource.

B. Combine each pair of simple sentences below into a compound sentence.

1. The Pacific Ocean is the largest ocean in the world.
It covers more area than all the earth's land put together.

_____

_____

2. Bodies of saltwater that are smaller than oceans are called seas, gulfs, or bays.
These bodies of water are often encircled by land.

_____

_____

3. Seas, gulfs, and bays are joined to the oceans.
They vary in size and depth.

_____

_____

4. The Mediterranean is one of the earth's largest seas.
It is almost entirely encircled by the southern part of Europe, the northern part of Africa, and the western part of Asia.

_____

_____

_____

Correcting Run-on Sentences

> ■ Two or more sentences run together without the correct punctuation are called a **run-on sentence.**
>   EXAMPLE: It will rain today, it will be sunny tomorrow.
> ■ One way to correct a run-on sentence is to separate it into two sentences.
>   EXAMPLE: It will rain today. It will be sunny tomorrow.
> ■ Another way to correct a run-on sentence is to separate the two main parts with a comma and <u>and</u>, <u>or</u>, <u>but</u>, <u>nor</u>, or <u>yet</u>.
>   EXAMPLE: It will rain today, but it will be sunny tomorrow.

■ **Rewrite each run-on sentence correctly.**

1. In 1860, the Pony Express started in St. Joseph, Missouri the route began where the railroads ended.

   _____

   _____

2. People in the West wanted faster mail service, the mail took six weeks by boat.

   _____

   _____

3. Mail sent by stagecoach took about 21 days, the Pony Express averaged ten days.

   _____

   _____

4. The Pony Express used a relay system riders and horses were switched at 157 places along the way to Sacramento, California.

   _____

   _____

5. Because teenagers weighed less than adults, most of the riders were teenagers the horses could run faster carrying them.

   _____

   _____

6. Riders had to cross raging rivers, the mountains were another barrier.

   _____

   _____

Expanding Sentences

> ■ Sentences can be **expanded** by adding details to make them clearer and more interesting.
>   EXAMPLE: The child waved. The child **in the blue hat** waved **timidly to me.**
> ■ Details added to sentences may answer these questions: When? (today) Where? (at home) How? (slowly) How often? (daily) To what degree? (very) What kind? (big) Which? (smallest) How many? (five)

A. Expand each sentence by adding details to answer the questions shown in parentheses. Write the expanded sentence on the line.

1. The ball soared.   (What kind? Where?)

   _____

2. It crashed.   (How? Where?)

   _____

3. It rolled.   (When? Where?)

   _____

4. I felt.   (How? To what degree?)

   _____

B. Decide how each of the following sentences can be expanded. Write your new sentence on the line.

1. The spaceship landed. _____

   _____

2. Out jumped a spacewoman. _____

   _____

3. The spacewoman talked. _____

   _____

4. I couldn't understand her words. _____

   _____

5. I ran and hid. _____

   _____

6. The spacewoman disappeared. _____

   _____

A. Label each sentence as follows: Write $\underline{D}$ if it is declarative, $\underline{IN}$ if it is interrogative, $\underline{IM}$ if it is imperative, and $\underline{E}$ if it is exclamatory. Write $\underline{X}$ if the group of words is not a sentence. Punctuate each sentence correctly.

_____ **1.** What is your favorite radio station____

_____ **2.** The one I listen to is having a contest____

_____ **3.** Call this number to win a prize____

_____ **4.** If you are the seventh caller____

_____ **5.** The winner will be announced immediately____

_____ **6.** I just won____

B. Draw a line between the complete subject and the complete predicate in each sentence below. Underline the simple subject once. Underline the simple predicate twice.

1. You must guess the number of beans that are in the jar.

2. John will write his guesses on these pieces of paper.

3. On the counter can be found pencils.

4. Melissa has already written her guess.

5. One of the sentences above is in inverted order. Rewrite that sentence in natural order on the line below.

_____

C. Label each sentence below as follows: Write $\underline{CS}$ if it has a compound subject, $\underline{CP}$ if it has a compound predicate, $\underline{C}$ if it is compound sentence, and $\underline{R}$ if it is a run-on sentence.

_____ **1.** Contestants buy something and fill out a form.

_____ **2.** Rules and dates for a contest are often printed on the entry form.

_____ **3.** I think of contests as challenging, and I often enter them.

_____ **4.** Sometimes I win contests I sometimes lose, too.

D. Expand each sentence below by inserting details. Write your expanded sentence on the blank lines.

1. The contest was won by a woman. _____

_____

2. She had filled out an entry form and sent in a jingle. _____

_____

3. The judges agreed that her entry was creative. _____

_____

A. Write complete sentences with each group of words below. In each sentence, underline the simple subject once and the simple predicate twice.

1. when I speak in front of people

   _____

2. the noise from the street

   _____

3. on the way to school this morning

   _____

4. a long way from home

   _____

5. had a birthday party for Diane

   _____

B. Complete each sentence below to make the kind of sentence named. Be sure to use the correct end punctuation.

1. **Declarative** The solar system consists of _____

2. **Interrogative** Which is the largest _____

3. **Imperative** Tell the class _____

4. **Exclamatory** What an enormous _____

C. To each compound subject or compound predicate below, add whatever words are needed to make a sentence.

1. _____ arrived at the game and sat in their seats.

2. _____ swept the plate and cried, "Play ball!"

3. The batter and pitcher _____.

4. _____ swung at and missed the ball.

5. The pitcher and the catcher _____.

6. _____ hit the ball and ran the bases.

D. Write two sentences in inverted order.

_____

_____

E. Rewrite the sentences below, making one of these improvements: (a) combine sentences by using compound subjects or compound predicates; (b) combine simple sentences to make compound sentences; (c) correct run-on sentences.

1. To take a good photograph, you need a good eye you do not need an expensive camera.

_____

_____

2. You just load your camera then you go for a walk.

_____

3. You may see something that is different. You may see something that is colorful.

_____

4. Perhaps you like the shape of an object or maybe you like the texture of an object.

_____

_____

5. Don't take your picture yet be sure your lens cap is off and your camera is focused correctly.

_____

_____

6. Think about what you do not want in your picture. Think about the way you want to frame your picture.

_____

_____

7. Take your time. Keep your camera steady.

_____

F. Expand each sentence below by adding details that make it clearer and more interesting.

1. The traffic roars on the highway.

_____

2. Cars move in and out of the lanes.

_____

3. Trucks go past small cars.

_____

Nouns

> ■ A **noun** is a word that names a person, place, thing, or quality.
> EXAMPLES: boy, Maria, river, Wyoming, house, beach, joy

A. Write nouns that name the following:

1. Four famous people

_____   _____

_____   _____

2. Four types of jobs

_____   _____

_____   _____

3. Four places you would like to visit

_____   _____

_____   _____

4. Four vegetables

_____   _____

_____   _____

5. Four qualities you would like to possess

_____   _____

_____   _____

B. Underline each noun.

1. Alaska is rich in gold, silver, copper, and oil.
2. Chocolate is made from the beans of a tree that grows in the tropics.
3. The distance across Texas is greater than the distance from Chicago to New York.
4. The boys and girls carried their pets in the parade.
5. The oldest city in California is San Diego.
6. Alexander Graham Bell, the inventor of the telephone, was born in Edinburgh, Scotland.
7. Jack, Diane, and I took a plane to London, where we saw Buckingham Palace.
8. Many interesting animals, such as piranhas, alligators, anacondas, and sloths, live in the Amazon River Basin.
9. The tarantula is a type of large, hairy spider.
10. The Maya were a people who lived in what is now Mexico and Central America.

Common and Proper Nouns

> - There are two main types of nouns: **common nouns** and **proper nouns.**
> - A **common noun** names any one of a class of objects.
>   EXAMPLES: girl, state, author
> - A **proper noun** is the name of a particular person, place, or thing. A proper noun begins with a capital letter.
>   EXAMPLES: Mark Twain, Tennessee, Washington Monument

A. Write a proper noun suggested by each common noun.

1. college _____
2. river _____
3. governor _____
4. singer _____
5. physician _____
6. holiday _____
7. TV show _____
8. city _____
9. teacher _____
10. classmate _____

11. car _____
12. school _____
13. lake _____
14. country _____
15. street _____
16. park _____
17. month _____
18. actor _____
19. girl _____
20. state _____

B. Write a common noun suggested by each proper noun.

1. Alaska _____
2. South America _____
3. Tuesday _____
4. Nile _____
5. Dr. Washington _____
6. Lake Superior _____
7. Thanksgiving _____
8. Pacific _____
9. Arizona _____
10. David _____

11. Mars _____
12. George Bush _____
13. February _____
14. Rocky Mountains _____
15. Mexico _____
16. *Treasure Island* _____
17. Jennifer _____
18. Detroit _____
19. Washington, D.C. _____
20. Fido _____

C. Underline each common noun.

1. The sturdy <u>timber</u> of the <u>oak</u> is used in constructing <u>furniture</u>, <u>bridges</u>, and <u>ships</u>.

2. Robert Fulton was a painter, jeweler, farmer, engineer, and inventor.

3. The main crops of Puerto Rico are sugar, tobacco, coffee, and fruits.

4. The pecan groves of Texas provide nuts for the eastern part of our country.

5. Michigan has many rivers, waterfalls, and lakes.

6. The Verrazano-Narrows Bridge between Brooklyn and Staten Island is the longest suspension bridge in the world.

7. Some of the main foods eaten in Greece are lamb, fish, olives, and feta cheese.

8. A road passes through a tunnel cut in the base of a giant tree in California.

9. Since the earliest civilizations, gold has been used for ornaments.

10. One of our largest lakes is Lake Erie.

11. The orange tree bears beautiful blossoms and delicious fruits.

12. Rockefeller Center is a large business and entertainment center in New York.

13. Pine trees give us turpentine, tar, resin, timber, and oils.

14. The United States buys the greatest amount of the world's coffee.

15. The pelican, the penguin, and the flamingo are interesting birds.

16. The first trip into space was filled with danger.

D. Underline each proper noun.

1. The principal crops grown in the United States are apples, corn, cotton, oats, peaches, potatoes, rice, rye, and wheat.

2. William Penn was the founder of Pennsylvania.

3. On the shelves of the Elm Grove Library, you will find many magical stories.

4. Commander Byrd, a naval officer, made the first airplane flight to the North Pole.

5. Dr. Jeanne Spurlock went to Howard University College of Medicine.

6. The orange tree was brought to Europe from Asia.

7. Colombia is the world's leading producer of emeralds.

8. Kilimanjaro is the tallest mountain in Africa.

9. The Navajo Indians make beautiful silver and turquoise jewelry.

10. Leticia and Carlos anchored the tent while Sam and Ted prepared the food.

11. Thomas Jefferson introduced the decimal system of coinage (dollars, dimes, cents) that we now use.

12. Their home is on the shore of Lake Michigan.

13. Quebec is the only city in North America that has a wall around it.

14. Paul Revere was a patriot, a silversmith, an engraver, and a dentist.

15. Lemons were first grown in the valleys of India.

16. The Sears Tower in Chicago is the tallest building in the world.

Singular and Plural Nouns

> ■ A **singular noun** names one person, place, or thing.
>   EXAMPLES: girl, half, pear, sky
> ■ A **plural noun** names more than one person, place, or thing.
>   EXAMPLES: girls, halves, pears, skies
> ■ Add -s to most nouns to make them plural.
>   EXAMPLES: girl, girls   top, tops
> ■ Add -es to most nouns ending in -ch, -sh, -s, or -x to make them plural.
>   EXAMPLES: church, churches   brush, brushes   ax, axes
> ■ If a noun ends in a consonant and -y, change the -y to -i and add -es.
>   EXAMPLES: city, cities   army, armies
> ■ If a noun ends in a vowel and -y, add -s to make it plural.
>   EXAMPLE: boy, boys

A. Write the plural form for each noun below.

1. newspaper _____

2. guess _____

3. town _____

4. valley _____

5. body _____

6. book _____

7. bush _____

8. office _____

9. tax _____

10. toy _____

11. boss _____

12. school _____

13. day _____

14. copy _____

15. author _____

16. porch _____

B. Complete each sentence with the plural form of the noun in parentheses.

1. (penny)   How many _____ make a dollar?

2. (dress)   Marcy makes all of her own_____.

3. (bridge)   How many _____ were destroyed by the flood?

4. (brush)   Mr. Perez got two new _____ yesterday.

5. (county)   How many _____ are there in your state?

6. (fox)   Seven _____ live at the zoo.

7. (story)   I like to read _____ about our pioneers.

8. (lunch)   She made several _____ before school.

9. (country)   How many _____ are there in South America?

- Some nouns ending in -f or -fe are made plural by changing the -f or -fe to -ves.
    - EXAMPLES: loaf, loaves   wife, wives
- Some nouns ending in -f are made plural by adding -s.
    - EXAMPLES: roof, roofs   bluff, bluffs
- Most nouns ending in -o that have a vowel just before the -o are made plural by adding -s.
    - EXAMPLE: radio, radios
- Some nouns ending in -o preceded by a consonant are made plural by adding -es, but others are made plural by adding only -s.
    - EXAMPLES: potato, potatoes   piano, pianos
- A few nouns have irregular plural forms.
    - EXAMPLES: child, children   man, men   ox, oxen
- A few nouns have the same form for both the singular and plural.
    - EXAMPLES: trout, trout   sheep, sheep

C. Write the plural form for each noun below. You might wish to check the spellings in a dictionary.

1. knife _____

2. loaf _____

3. half _____

4. mouse _____

5. foot _____

6. goose _____

7. hoof _____

8. moose _____

9. life _____

10. tomato _____

11. tooth _____

12. piano _____

D. Complete each sentence with the plural form of the word in parentheses. You may wish to check the spellings in a dictionary.

1. (foot)   My new shoes pinch my _____.

2. (sheep)   The shepherd always takes good care of the _____.

3. (chimney)   Many _____ were blown down during the recent storm.

4. (city)   Many _____ are establishing recreation centers.

5. (leaf)   The high winds scattered the dead _____ over the yard.

6. (Mosquito)   _____ breed wherever there is standing water.

7. (nickel)   I have five Jefferson _____.

8. (friend)   Her _____ arrived on the bus yesterday.

9. (desk)   New _____ have been ordered for our office.

10. (bench)   Concrete _____ have been placed along the walk.

Possessive Nouns

> - A **possessive noun** shows possession of the noun that follows.
> - Form the possessive of most singular nouns by adding an apostrophe (') and -s.
>   EXAMPLES: the boy's hat   Mr. Thomas's car
> - Form the possessive of a plural noun ending in -s by adding only an apostrophe.
>   EXAMPLES: the Smiths' home   girls' bikes   sisters' names
> - Form the possessive of a plural noun that does not end in -s by adding an apostrophe and -s.
>   EXAMPLES: children's classes   men's books

A. Write the possessive form of each noun.

1. girl _____girl's_____

2. child _____

3. women _____

4. children _____

5. John _____

6. baby _____

7. boys _____

8. teacher _____

9. Dr. Ray _____

10. ladies _____

11. brother _____

12. soldier _____

13. men _____

14. aunt _____

15. Mrs. Jones _____

B. Rewrite each phrase using a possessive noun.

1. the cap belonging to Jim _____Jim's cap_____

2. the wrench that belongs to Kathy _____

3. the smile of the baby _____

4. the car that my parents own _____

5. the new shoes that belong to Kim _____

6. the collar of the dog _____

7. the golf clubs that Frank owns _____

8. the shoes that belong to the runners _____

9. the friends of our parents _____

10. the opinion of the editor _____

11. the lunches of the children _____

12. the coat belonging to Kyle _____

13. the assignment of the teacher _____

C. Complete each sentence with the possessive form of the word in parentheses.

1. (company) The _____ picnic will be at the park Saturday afternoon.

2. (dog) That _____ owner should pay for the damage it did.

3. (women) The _____ organization planned the meeting.

4. (Doug) _____ account of his trip was very interesting.

5. (David) _____ explanation of the problem was very clear.

6. (cat) My _____ eyes are blue.

7. (Kurt) _____ brother made the candy for our party.

8. (Men) _____ coats are sold at the store in that block.

9. (squirrel) The _____ teeth were very sharp.

10. (brother) We want to go to his _____ ranch.

11. (child) A _____ toy was found in our yard.

12. (horses) The _____ manes were smooth and shiny.

13. (baby) That dog played with the _____ shoe.

14. (teachers) Her _____ names are Miss Gomez and Mr. Jacobs.

15. (Alex) We are going to _____ party tomorrow.

16. (deer) They saw a _____ tracks in the snow.

17. (Stacy) _____ work is the neatest I have ever seen.

18. (country) We display our _____ flag every day.

19. (robins) I have heard those _____ calls every day this week.

20. (person) That _____ speech was much too long.

21. (sister) Nickie wants to go to her _____ graduation.

22. (children) The _____ parade is held every spring.

23. (neighbors) Our _____ yards have just been mowed.

24. (class) It is this _____ time to take the test.

25. (boys) This store sells _____ clothes.

26. (designer) The _____ exhibit won first place.

27. (horse) The _____ mane is black.

Appositives

> - An **appositive** is a noun or phrase that identifies or explains the noun it follows.
> - Use a comma before and after an appositive. If an appositive is at the end of a sentence, use a comma before it.
>   EXAMPLES: Jenna is graduating from Spring Hill, **her junior high school.**
>   Christoper's baseball team, **the Padres,** won every game they played.

A. Circle the appositive in each sentence. Underline the noun it identifies or explains.

1. Aunt Ruth, a good cook, invited us to dinner.

2. She lives on a small lane, Tinkerway.

3. Uncle Max, her husband, showed us magic tricks.

4. Aunt Ruth served her specialty, broiled chicken.

5. Mom brought dessert, a fresh strawberry pie.

6. Carol and Ron, our cousins, brought out a game.

7. But Scamp, their new puppy, wanted to play.

8. Uncle Max threw Scamp's toy, a red ball.

9. Scamp, their beagle, chased the ball under the chair.

10. The pup ran under the bed, a favorite hiding place.

B. Write sentences using the appositives below.

1. the cleanest room in the house ___Our living room, the cleanest room in the house, is___

___usually kept for entertaining company.___

2. the most interesting teacher _____

_____

3. the best day of the week _____

_____

4. my favorite sport _____

_____

5. a movie star _____

_____

6. a tropical island _____

_____

Verbs

> ■ A **verb** is a word that expresses action, being, or state of being.
> EXAMPLES: Helen **went** to school. These books **are** yours.
> Elizabeth and Paul **sing** in the school choir.

■ **Underline the verb in each sentence.**

1. Where **are** the Rocky Mountains?

2. W. C. Handy **wrote** "Saint Louis Blues."

3. **Check** your papers carefully.

4. Bananas **have** great food value.

5. Africa **is** the home of the hippopotamus.

6. The car **reached** the narrow bridge.

7. Gwendolyn Brooks **won** a Pulitzer Prize.

8. Elizabeth's father **trains** good mechanics.

9. Sue **has** a black puppy.

10. How many stars **are** on our flag?

11. The people of our town **remember** the cold winter.

12. Peter Minuit **bought** Manhattan Island for about twenty-four dollars.

13. What **is** your favorite book?

14. They **followed** the old trail to the top of the hill.

15. The wind **whistled** around the corner.

16. Eric always **watches** the news.

17. Their team **scored** twice in the third quarter.

18. Which driver **won** the auto race?

19. The third house from the corner **is** white.

20. Mexico **is** our southern neighbor.

21. Tom **set** the table for five people.

22. **Answer** my question.

23. Mrs. Sung **explained** how the computer **operates.**

24. Jason **worked** in the flower bed for his grandfather.

25. Our town **has** a public swimming pool.

26. My brother **plays** the saxophone.

27. **Brush** your teeth frequently.

28. A puff of wind **whirled** the leaves over the lawn.

29. We **arrived** at our camp early in the morning.

30. Where **is** the launching pad?

Unit 3, Grammar and Usage   35

> ■ Some sentences contain a **verb phrase.** A verb phrase consists of a
> **main verb** and one or more other verbs.
> EXAMPLES: The girls **are singing.** Where **have** you **been?**

■ **Underline the verb or verb phrase in each sentence.**

1. The first American schools were held in homes.

2. Who invented the jet engine?

3. *The New England Primer* was the earliest American textbook.

4. John Philip Sousa was a bandmaster and composer.

5. Who built the first motorcycle?

6. My friends will arrive on Saturday afternoon.

7. What was the final score?

8. Ryan has made this unusual birdhouse.

9. The waves covered the beach with many shells.

10. I have ridden on a motor scooter.

11. The artist is molding clay.

12. Beverly and her parents spent last summer in the Ozarks.

13. The names of the new employees are posted by the supervisor.

14. Paul has found a new hat.

15. She is going to the store.

16. We have trimmed the hedges.

17. Our nation exports many kinds of food.

18. My friend is reading a book about the Civil War.

19. Jane Addams helped many foreign-born people in Chicago.

20. Oil was discovered in West Texas.

21. Jenny Lind was called the Swedish Nightingale.

22. We are planning a car trip to Miami.

23. That dog has howled for two hours.

24. Our guests have arrived.

25. I have written letters to several companies.

26. I can name two important cities in this state.

27. The hummingbird received its name because of the sound of its wings.

28. Jan's poem was printed in the newspaper.

29. Charles and Adam are working at the hamburger stand.

30. This table was painted recently.

Helping Verbs

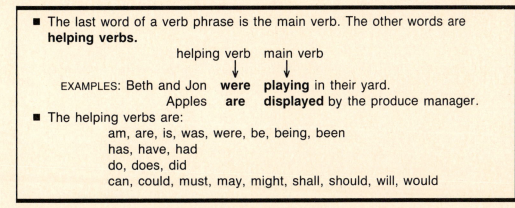

- The last word of a verb phrase is the main verb. The other words are **helping verbs.**

                        helping verb   main verb
                              ↓   ↓
    EXAMPLES: Beth and Jon **were** **playing** in their yard.
                    Apples **are** **displayed** by the produce manager.

- The helping verbs are:
    am, are, is, was, were, be, being, been
    has, have, had
    do, does, did
    can, could, must, may, might, shall, should, will, would

A. Underline the verb phrase, and circle the helping verb in each sentence below.

1. Mom and Dad (have) begun their spring cleaning.

2. Molly and Anne will rake the leaves on the front lawn.

3. Vincent and April must sweep the driveway.

4. The twins, Dawn and Daniela, will pull the weeds.

5. Christopher and his cousin, Lisa, may prepare lunch for the workers.

6. They should wash their hands first.

7. Sandwiches and fruit salad would make a delicious lunch on a hot day.

8. Our next-door neighbor is working on his lawn, too.

9. He has sprayed his front and back lawns with a fertilizer.

10. Every helper must close the garbage bags tightly.

11. Squirrels, raccoons, and large crows would enjoy our garbage.

12. We might finish the outside work today.

B. Use each verb phrase in a sentence.

1. would come _____

2. should choose _____

3. had bought _____

4. might find _____

5. am writing _____

6. will learn _____

7. could become _____

8. were standing _____

More Helping Verbs

> ■ A verb phrase may have more than one helping verb.
>
>   helping verb   main verb
>
>   ↓   ↓
>
>   EXAMPLES: Bill **should have** **taken** the bus to school.
>
>   My tomato plants **have been** **growing** very quickly.
>
> ■ In a question or a sentence containing a word such as <u>not</u> or <u>never</u>, the helping verb might be separated from the main verb.
>
>   EXAMPLES: When **will** you **decide** to fix your bicycle?
>
>   Jason **has** not **fixed** his bicycle.

A. Underline the verb phrases, and circle the helping verbs in the sentences below.

1. Our final exam (will be) given on May 10.

2. Many students have been studying every night.

3. My friends and I may be forming a study group.

4. The study group members should be reviewing each chapter.

5. Are you joining our study group?

6. May we meet in your house one afternoon next week?

7. Kim and Tim should have known the answers to the first ten questions.

8. Where have you been all day?

9. I have been looking everywhere for you.

10. I would have met you earlier.

11. The airplane flight has been delayed in Chicago.

12. Would you prefer an earlier flight?

13. No, I had been enjoying a long visit with my grandmother.

14. My parents have been waiting for over two hours in the airport.

15. Lois and Jeanine had been at the pool all day.

16. Will any other friends be swimming in the pool?

17. Several neighborhood children must have been splashing each other.

18. Could Jessica and I take diving lessons next summer?

B. Use each verb phrase in a statement.

1. should have bought _____

2. had been finished _____

C. Use each verb phrase in a question.

1. will be going _____

2. have been practicing _____

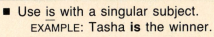

> - Use <u>is</u> with a singular subject.
>   EXAMPLE: Tasha **is** the winner.
> - Use <u>are</u> with a plural subject.
>   EXAMPLE: The boys **are** walking home.
> - Always use are with the pronoun <u>you</u>.
>   EXAMPLE: You **are** absolutely right!

A. Underline the correct verb to complete each sentence.

1. (Is, Are) this tool ready to be cleaned?

2. The boys (is, are) making peanut brittle.

3. Bill (is, are) the chairperson this week.

4. Where (is, are) my gloves?

5. This tomato (is, are) too ripe.

6. Ryan, (is, are) these your books?

7. Mother, (is, are) the sandwiches ready?

8. (Is, Are) you going to sing your solo this morning?

9. This newspaper (is, are) the early edition.

10. Carol asked if you (is, are) still coming to the game.

> - Use <u>was</u> with a singular subject to tell about the past.
>   EXAMPLE: I **was** there yesterday.
> - Use <u>were</u> with a plural subject to tell about the past.
>   EXAMPLE: Kevin and Ray **were** not home.
> - Always use <u>were</u> with the pronoun <u>you</u>.
>   EXAMPLE: You **were** only a few minutes late.

B. Underline the correct verb to complete each sentence.

1. Amy and Crystal (was, were) disappointed because they could not go.

2. Our seats (was, were) near the stage.

3. Taro, Bill, and Luis (was, were) assigned to the first team.

4. These puppets (was, were) made by a company in Chicago.

5. There (was, were) only one carton of milk in the refrigerator.

6. Who (was, were) that person on the corner?

7. She (was, were) at my house this morning.

8. You (was, were) the best swimmer in the contest.

9. Those tomatoes (was, were) delicious!

10. He (was, were) late for school today.

Verb Tenses

- The **tense** of a verb tells the time of the action or being.
- **Present tense** tells that something is happening now.
  EXAMPLES: Mandy **dances** in the show. My piano lessons **start** today.
- **Past tense** tells that something happened in the past. The action is over.
  EXAMPLES: Mandy **danced** in the show.
  My piano lessons **started** last June.
- **Future tense** tells that something will happen in the future. Use <u>will</u>
  with the verb.
  EXAMPLES: Mandy **will dance** in the show.
  My piano lessons **will start** next month.

A. Underline the verb or verb phrase in each sentence. Then write <u>present</u>, <u>past</u>, or <u>future</u> for the tense of each verb.

1. My aunt, uncle, and cousins live in a house near mine. _____

2. Sometimes I care for my cousins, Karen and Billy. _____

3. They play in front of my house. _____

4. One day Karen threw the ball very hard to Billy. _____

5. The ball sailed over Billy's head and into the street. _____

6. Billy ran toward the street _____

7. I shouted to Billy. _____

8. Usually, Billy listens to me. _____

9. I got the ball from the street. _____

10. Billy's mom called for him to come home. _____

11. He went as fast as possible. _____

12. Next time they will play only in the backyard. _____

B. Rewrite each sentence, changing the underlined verb to the past tense.

1. My little sister <u>will follow</u> me everywhere.

_____

2. She <u>comes</u> to my friend's house.

_____

3. She <u>rides</u> my bicycle on the grass.

_____

Principal Parts of Verbs

- A verb has four principal parts: **present, present participle, past,** and **past participle.**
- For **regular verbs,** the present participle is formed by adding -ing to the present. It is used with a form of the helping verb be.
- The past and past participles are formed by adding -ed to the present. The past participle uses a form of the helping verb have.

  EXAMPLES:

Present	Present Participle	Past	Past Participle
walk	(is) walking	walked	(have, has, had) walked
point	(is) pointing	pointed	(have, has, had) pointed
cook	(is) cooking	cooked	(have, has, had) cooked

- **Irregular verbs** form their past and past participles in other ways. A dictionary shows the principal parts of these verbs.

- Write the present participle, past, and past participle for each verb.

PRESENT	PRESENT PARTICIPLE	PAST	PAST PARTICIPLE
1. walk	(is) walking	walked	(have, has, had) walked
2. visit			
3. watch			
4. follow			
5. jump			
6. talk			
7. add			
8. learn			
9. paint			
10. plant			
11. work			
12. divide			
13. miss			
14. score			
15. call			
16. collect			

Past Tenses of *See, Do,* and *Come*

- Never use a helping verb with: <u>saw</u>   <u>did</u>   <u>came</u>
- Always use a helping verb with: <u>seen</u>   <u>done</u>   <u>come</u>

- **Underline the correct verb form to complete each sentence.**

  1. We (saw, seen) the carnival.

  2. Suddenly, the whole idea (came, come) to me.

  3. Tammy and John (did, done) not do the ironing this morning.

  4. The children (saw, seen) that a lot of work had to be done to the camp.

  5. Who (did, done) the framing of these prints?

  6. The rain (came, come) down in sheets.

  7. I haven't (did, done) all the errands for Aunt Anna.

  8. I have (came, come) to help arrange the stage.

  9. We have (saw, seen) many miles of beautiful prairie flowers.

  10. What have you (did, done) with the kittens?

  11. My uncle (came, come) to help me move.

  12. I have not (saw, seen) the new apartment today.

  13. Why haven't your brothers (came, come) to help us?

  14. Haven't you ever (saw, seen) a spider spinning a web?

  15. When Lynne and I (came, come) in, we found a surprise.

  16. I (saw, seen) the owner about the job.

  17. We saw what you (did, done)!

  18. Has the mail (came, come) yet?

  19. The prettiest place we (saw, seen) was the Grand Canyon.

  20. Hasn't Kyle (did, done) a nice job of painting the room?

  21. Mr. Lopez (came, come) to repair the stove.

  22. My dog, Max, (did, done) that trick twice.

  23. Josh hadn't (came, come) to the soccer game.

  24. Rebecca (saw, seen) the movie yesterday.

  25. Scott has (came, come) to the picnic.

  26. Who has (saw, seen) the Rocky Mountains?

  27. Deb (did, done) the decorations for the party.

  28. She (came, come) to the party an hour early.

  29. The bird (saw, seen) the cat near the tree.

  30. The painter has (did, done) a nice job on the house.

Past Tenses of *Eat* and *Drink*

> - Never use a helping verb with: <u>ate</u>   <u>drank</u>
> - Always use a helping verb with: <u>eaten</u>   <u>drunk</u>

A. Underline the correct verb form to complete each sentence.

1. Have the worms (ate, eaten) the leaves on that tree?

2. We (drank, drunk) the spring water from the mountains.

3. You (ate, eaten) more for breakfast than I did.

4. Haven't you (drank, drunk) a glass of this refreshing lemonade?

5. The hungry hikers (ate, eaten) quickly.

6. Yes, I (drank, drunk) two glasses of lemonade.

7. Have you (ate, eaten) your lunch so soon?

8. Maggie, why haven't you (drank, drunk) your milk?

9. I (ate, eaten) two delicious hamburgers for lunch.

10. We watched the birds as they (drank, drunk) from the birdbath.

11. We (ate, eaten) supper early.

12. Who (drank, drunk) a glass of tomato juice?

13. Have you ever (ate, eaten) a pink grapefruit?

14. Elizabeth, have you (drank, drunk) an extra glass of milk?

15. Have you (ate, eaten) your breakfast yet?

16. Yes, I (drank, drunk) it about noon.

B. Write the correct past tense form of each verb in parentheses to complete each sentence.

1. (eat) Maria had _____ turkey and stuffing at Thanksgiving.

2. (drink) She _____ cranberry juice for breakfast.

3. (eat) Carlos _____ a second sandwich.

4. (drink) At the picnic we had _____ a gallon of lemonade.

5. (drink) Yes, I _____ it at about noon.

6. (eat) Cory hasn't _____ since breakfast.

7. (drink) Father _____ a glass of iced tea.

8. (eat) Did you know that those apples had been _____?

9. (drink) Haven't Mike and Lisa _____ the fresh orange juice?

10. (eat) The people on the train _____ in the dining car.

> - Never use a helping verb with: <u>sang</u> <u>rang</u>
> - Always use a helping verb with: <u>sung</u> <u>rung</u>

A. Underline the correct verb form to complete each sentence.

1. I have never (sang, sung) in public before.

2. Have the church bells (rang, rung)?

3. The group (sang, sung) all their college songs for us.

4. The bell had not (rang, rung) at five o'clock.

5. The children (sang, sung) three patriotic songs.

6. We (rang, rung) their doorbell several times.

7. Which of the three sisters (sang, sung) in the talent show?

8. Who (rang, rung) the outside bell?

9. Patti, have you ever (sang, sung) for the choir director?

10. I (rang, rung) the large old bell that is beside the door.

11. Has she ever (sang, sung) this duet?

12. The Liberty Bell hasn't (rang, rung) in many years.

13. The girls (sang, sung) as they had never (sang, sung) before.

14. The ship's bell hasn't (rang, rung).

15. The Canadian singer often (sang, sung) that song.

16. Have you (rang, rung) the bell on that post?

B. Write the correct past tense form of the verb in parentheses to complete each sentence.

1. (ring) It was so noisy that we couldn't tell if the bell had _____.

2. (sing) Maria _____ a solo.

3. (sing) She had never _____ alone before.

4. (ring) The bells _____ to announce their marriage yesterday.

5. (ring) Have you _____ the bell yet?

6. (sing) Who _____ the first song?

7. (ring) The group _____ bells to play a tune.

8. (sing) Hasn't she _____ before royalty?

9. (ring) The boxer jumped up as the bell _____.

10. (sing) That young boy _____ a solo.

> ■ Never use a helping verb with: <u>froze</u> <u>chose</u> <u>spoke</u> <u>broke</u>
> ■ Always use a helping verb with: <u>frozen</u> <u>chosen</u> <u>spoken</u> <u>broken</u>

A. Underline the correct verb form to complete each sentence.

1. Haven't those candidates (spoke, spoken) yet?

2. Has the dessert (froze, frozen) in the molds?

3. I (broke, broken) the handle of the hammer.

4. Have you (spoke, spoken) to your friends about the meeting?

5. Hadn't the coach (chose, chosen) the best players today?

6. The dog has (broke, broken) the toy.

7. Has Anna (spoke, spoken) to you about going with us?

8. We (froze, frozen) the ice for our picnic.

9. I believe you (chose, chosen) the right clothes.

10. Dave, haven't you (broke, broken) your bat?

11. Mr. Mann (spoke, spoken) first.

12. Mother (froze, frozen) the fruit salad for our picnic.

13. You didn't tell me he had (broke, broken) his arm.

14. The boys on the team (chose, chosen) their captain.

15. Mrs. Ramirez (spoke, spoken) first.

16. Has the river (froze, frozen) yet?

B. Write the correct past tense form of the verb in parentheses to complete each sentence.

1. (freeze)   We could not tell if the ice had _____ overnight.

2. (break)   The chain on Ann's bicycle had _____ while she rode.

3. (choose)   Carol had _____ to be in the play.

4. (speak)   No one _____ while the band played.

5. (choose)   Tom has _____ to take both tests today.

6. (choose)   Jim _____ not to take the test early.

7. (break)   No one knew who had _____ the window.

8. (speak)   Carol _____ her lines loudly and clearly.

9. (freeze)   It was so cold that everything had _____.

10. (speak)   The teacher wanted to know who had _____ in the library.

■ Never use a helping verb with: <u>knew</u> <u>grew</u> <u>threw</u>
■ Always use a helping verb with: <u>known</u> <u>grown</u> <u>thrown</u>

A. Underline the correct verb form to complete each sentence.

1. We have (knew, known) her family for years.

2. Weeds (grew, grown) along the park paths.

3. Hasn't Julia (threw, thrown) the softball?

4. I have never (knew, known) a more courageous person.

5. Katie has (grew, grown) very rapidly.

6. How many times have you (threw, thrown) at the target?

7. Has Mrs. Paggi (grew, grown) any unusual plants this year?

8. I (knew, known) every person at the meeting.

9. I wish that my hair hadn't (grew, grown) so much this year.

10. Brian, how long have you (knew, known) Lee?

11. The pitcher has (threw, thrown) three strikes in a row.

12. I don't know why the plants (grew, grown) so fast.

13. We (threw, thrown) out many old boxes.

14. Mr. Low has (grew, grown) vegetables this summer.

15. Marty (knew, known) the correct answer.

16. The guard (threw, thrown) the ball to the center.

17. She is the nicest person I have ever (knew, known).

18. The sun (grew, grown) brighter in the afternoon.

B. Write one original sentence with <u>knew</u>. Then write one sentence with <u>known</u>.

1. _____

2. _____

C. Write one original sentence with <u>grew</u>. Then write one sentence with <u>grown</u>.

1. _____

2. _____

D. Write one original sentence with <u>threw</u>. Then write one sentence with <u>thrown</u>.

1. _____

2. _____

Past Tenses of *Blow* and *Fly*

- Never use a helping verb with: <u>blew</u>   <u>flew</u>
- Always use a helping verb with: <u>blown</u>   <u>flown</u>

A. Underline the correct verb form to complete each sentence.

1. Flags (flew, flown) from many houses on the Fourth of July.

2. The train whistles have (blew, blown) at every crossing.

3. The birds haven't (flew, flown) south for the winter.

4. The wind (blew, blown) the kites to pieces.

5. The candles (blew, blown) out too soon.

6. Has your sister (flew, flown) her new kite?

7. Yes, she (flew, flown) it this morning.

8. All the papers have (blew, blown) across the floor.

9. Four boys (flew, flown) their model airplanes in the tournament.

10. The wind has (blew, blown) like this for an hour.

11. I didn't know that you had (flew, flown) here in a jet.

12. Hasn't the train whistle (blew, blown) yet?

13. The airplanes (flew, flown) in an aviation show.

14. Our largest maple tree had (blew, blown) down last night.

15. The striped hot-air balloon has (flew, flown) the farthest.

16. The judge (blew, blown) the whistle as the runner crossed the finish line.

17. The Carsons have (flew, flown) to Europe.

18. An erupting volcano (blew, blown) the mountain apart.

19. The geese (flew, flown) in formation.

20. The curtains have (blew, blown) open from the breeze.

21. The movie star (flew, flown) in a private jet.

22. A tornado (blew, blown) the roof off a house.

23. A pair of ducks has (flew, flown) overhead.

B. Write one original sentence with <u>blew</u>. Then write one sentence with <u>blown</u>.

1. _____

2. _____

C. Write one original sentence with <u>flew</u>. Then write one sentence with <u>flown</u>.

1. _____

2. _____

Past Tenses of *Take* and *Write*

- Never use a helping verb with: <u>took</u>   <u>wrote</u>
- Always use a helping verb with: <u>taken</u>   <u>written</u>

A. Underline the correct verb form to complete each sentence.

1. They (took, taken) the first plane to Tampa.

2. Who has (wrote, written) the best script for the play?

3. Mike hadn't (took, taken) these pictures last summer.

4. Who (wrote, written) the minutes of our last club meeting?

5. We (took, taken) down our paintings.

6. Marguerite Henry has (wrote, written) many stories about horses.

7. I (took, taken) my watch to the jeweler for repair.

8. I (wrote, written) for a video catalog.

9. Haven't you (took, taken) your medicine yet?

10. Diana, have you (wrote, written) to your grandmother?

11. Carlos (took, taken) too much time getting ready.

12. Diane hadn't (wrote, written) these exercises with a pen.

13. Who (took, taken) my magazine?

14. Mario (wrote, written) an excellent business letter.

B. Write the correct past tense form of the verb in parentheses to complete each sentence.

1. (write) Who _____ this short theme?

2. (take) It has _____ me a long time to make this planter.

3. (write) Eve Merriam had _____ this poem.

4. (take) The children have _____ off their muddy shoes.

5. (write) We _____ letters to our state senators.

6. (take) Louisa, have you _____ your brother for a walk?

7. (write) My cousin _____ me a letter about his new goldfish.

8. (write) Robert Frost _____ David's favorite poem.

9. (take) Willie and Sharon _____ the bus to the park.

10. (write) Mr. Bustos _____ an excellent article for our newspaper.

11. (take) The nurse _____ my temperature.

Past Tenses of *Give* and *Go*

- Never use a helping verb with: <u>gave</u> <u>went</u>
- Always use a helping verb with: <u>given</u> <u>gone</u>

A. Underline the correct verb form to complete each sentence.

1. Ms. Morris has (gave, given) that land to the city.

2. Where has Ann (went, gone) this afternoon?

3. Carlos (gave, given) a speech on collecting rare coins.

4. My brothers (went, gone) to the park an hour ago.

5. Mary, who (gave, given) you this ruby ring?

6. Rob and Carter have (went, gone) to paint the house.

7. Mr. Edwards (gave, given) us ten minutes to solve the problems.

8. Elaine has (went, gone) to help Eileen find the place.

9. My friends (gave, given) clothing to the people whose house burned.

10. Hasn't Jan (went, gone) to the store yet?

11. The sportscaster has just (gave, given) the latest baseball scores.

12. Charlie (went, gone) to apply for the job.

13. Have you (gave, given) Fluffy her food?

14. Has Miss Martinson (went, gone) to Springfield?

15. I have (gave, given) my horn to my cousin.

16. Paula has (went, gone) to sleep already.

B. Write the correct past tense form of the verb in parentheses to complete each sentence.

1. (go) Paula _____ to sleep already.

2. (give) Has Mrs. Tate _____ the checks to the other employees?

3. (go) Every person had _____ before you arrived.

4. (give) My neighbor was _____ a ticket for speeding.

5. (go) Haven't the Yamadas _____ to Japan for a month?

6. (give) Mrs. O'Malley has _____ me a notebook.

7. (go) Haven't you ever _____ to an aquarium?

8. (give) I _____ her my new address.

9. (go) Michael _____ to camp for a week.

10. (give) Ms. Rosen has _____ me driving lessons.

> - A **possessive pronoun** is a pronoun that shows ownership of something.
> - The possessive pronouns <u>hers</u>, <u>mine</u>, <u>ours</u>, <u>theirs</u>, and <u>yours</u> stand alone.
>   EXAMPLES: The coat is **mine**. The shoes are **yours**.
> - The possessive pronouns <u>her</u>, <u>its</u>, <u>my</u>, <u>our</u>, <u>their</u>, and <u>your</u> must be used before nouns.
>   EXAMPLES: **Her** car is red. **Our** car is black.
> - The pronoun <u>his</u> may be used either way.
>   EXAMPLES: That is **his** dog. The dog is **his**.

- **Underline the possessive pronoun in each sentence.**

1. Lora lost her bracelet.

2. David broke his arm.

3. The dogs wagged their tails.

4. The referee blew her whistle.

5. The children should take their books.

6. Musician Louis Armstrong was famous for his smile.

7. Brad entered his model airplane in the contest.

8. I wanted to read that book, but a number of its pages are missing.

9. My aunt and uncle have sold their Arizona ranch.

10. The Eskimos build their igloos out of snow blocks.

11. How did Florida get its name?

12. David showed the group his wonderful stamp collection.

13. Coffee found its way from Arabia to Java.

14. The magpie builds its nest very carefully.

15. Pam sprained her ankle while skiing.

16. Lisa drove her car to the top of the peak.

17. Frank left his raincoat in the doctor's office.

18. Isn't Alaska noted for its salmon?

19. Travis brought his mother a beautiful shawl from India.

20. Gina, where is your brother?

21. Manuel forgot about his appointment with the dentist.

22. The children have gone to their swimming lesson.

23. Sandra showed her report to the boss.

24. Juan gave his father a beautiful paperweight.

25. Mr. Owens found his keys.

26. The little girls broke their swing.

Indefinite Pronouns

- An **indefinite pronoun** is a pronoun that does not refer to a specific person or thing.
    EXAMPLES: **Someone** is coming to speak with the students.
    Does **anyone** know what time it is?
    Everybody is looking forward to the field trip.
- Some indefinite pronouns are negative.
    EXAMPLES: **Nobody** has a ticket.
    No one was waiting at the bus stop.
- The indefinite pronouns anybody, anyone, anything, each, everyone, everybody, everything, nobody, no one, nothing, somebody, someone, and something are singular. They take singular verbs.
    EXAMPLE: **Everyone is** ready.
- The indefinite pronouns both, few, many, several, and some are plural. They take plural verbs.
    EXAMPLE: **Several** of us **are** ready.

A. Underline the indefinite pronoun in each sentence below.

1. Everyone helped complete the project.
2. Is somebody waiting for you?
3. Anything is possible.
4. Something arrived in the mail.
5. Everybody looked tired at practice.
6. No one was willing to work longer.
7. Does anyone have a quarter?
8. Both of us were tired.
9. Nothing was dry yet.
10. Does anybody want to go swimming?
11. Someone should speak up.
12. Everybody is hungry now.
13. Each of the cats was black.
14. Some of the dogs bark all the time.
15. Several were empty.
16. No one remembered to bring it.
17. Everyone started to feel nervous.
18. Nobody admitted to being afraid.
19. Everything will be explained.
20. Is anything missing?

B. Complete each sentence with an indefinite pronoun.

1. I can't believe that _____ in my desk has disappeared.

2. Is _____ coming to teach you to run the computer?

3. Every person in our class attended today. _____ was absent.

4. She tried to call, but _____ answered the phone.

5. Does _____ remember the address?

6. There is _____ here to see you.

7. Would _____ like a piece of cake?

8. The party was so much fun. _____ enjoyed it.

Subject Pronouns

> - A **subject pronoun** is used as the subject or as part of the subject of a sentence.
> - The subject pronouns are I, you, he, she, it, we, and they.
>   EXAMPLE: **It** has beautiful wings.
> - When the pronoun I is used with nouns or other pronouns, it is always named last.
>   EXAMPLE: Marie and **I** caught a butterfly.

- **Underline the correct pronoun.**

   1. Madeline and (I, me) helped repair the car.

   2. (She, Her) is going to the studio.

   3. Why can't Leigh and (I, me) go with them?

   4. (She, Her) and Charles skated all afternoon.

   5. Jaclyn and (I, me) are going to Chicago tomorrow.

   6. (He, Him) played tennis this morning.

   7. Beth and (he, him) were five minutes late yesterday morning.

   8. (She, Her) and (I, me) spent an hour in the library.

   9. Grandmother and (I, me) worked until nine o'clock.

   10. (He, Him) and Yuri are going over there now.

   11. May (we, us) carry your packages?

   12. (They, Them) and I are buying some groceries.

   13. Sarah and (I, me) are going with her to the park.

   14. (It, Them) wagged its tail.

   15. (She, You) have a beautiful singing voice, Claire.

   16. (He, Him) is the owner of the suitcase.

   17. Crystal and (I, me) are on the same team.

   18. (She, Her) has started a book club.

   19. (We, Us) are planning a bike trip.

   20. (They, Them) are going to see a Shakespearean play.

   21. Is (she, her) your favorite singer?

   22. Martin and (I, me) would be happy to help you.

   23. (We, Us) work at the post office.

   24. Grandpa and (we, us) are painting the front porch.

   25. (He, Him) excels as a photographer.

   26. (She, Her) has known us for several years.

   27. (I, Me) am the director of the community choir.

> ■ An **object pronoun** is used after an action verb or a preposition, such as <u>after</u>, <u>against</u>, <u>at</u>, <u>between</u>, <u>except</u>, <u>for</u>, <u>from</u>, <u>in</u>, <u>of</u>, <u>to</u>, and <u>with</u>.
> ■ The object pronouns are <u>me</u>, <u>you</u>, <u>him</u>, <u>her</u>, <u>it</u>, <u>us</u>, and <u>them</u>.
>   EXAMPLE: The game was for **him.**
> ■ When the pronoun <u>me</u> is used with nouns or other pronouns, it is always last.
>   EXAMPLE: The books were for Kay and **me.**

■ **Underline the correct pronoun.**

1. Tony, are you going with Stephanie and (I, me) to see Rosa?

2. Scott invited Patrick and (I, me) to one of the club picnics.

3. I am going to see Mary and (she, her) about this problem.

4. The lady told (us, we) to come for her old magazines.

5. I went with Mrs. Krueger and (she, her) to the hobby show.

6. That dinner was prepared by (them, they).

7. Mr. Jones asked Andrew and (I, me) to the baseball game.

8. Emily and Bev congratulated (he, him).

9. Miss Carr praised (him, he) for his work.

10. Will you talk to (she, her) about the trip?

11. Ben, can you go with Renee and (I, me)?

12. Grandfather lectured (us, we) about being on time.

13. The package was leaning against (it, we).

14. They brought the problem to (we, us).

15. It was too hard for (they, them) to solve.

16. Richard gave (I, me) his old catcher's equipment.

17. Ms. Jackson is teaching (we, us) Morse code.

18. Please inform (he, him) of the change of plans.

19. Brian offered to help (I, me) hang the curtains.

20. That car belongs to (he, him).

21. Carl didn't see (they, them).

22. Nancy asked him to take a picture of (we, us).

23. Please wait for (she, her) after school.

24. She is in the Spanish club with (he, him).

25. Hand the packages to (they, them).

26. Was this really discovered by (she, her)?

27. Would you like to play basketball with (we, us)?

- A **linking verb** connects the subject of a sentence with a noun or adjective that comes after the linking verb.

  Subject   Linking Verb   Noun

  EXAMPLES: The **baby**   was   **Christopher.**

  The **piano players**   were   **my cousins.**

- Use a subject pronoun after a linking verb.

  EXAMPLES: The **baby**   was   **he.**

  The **piano players**   were   **they.**

- Use a subject pronoun after such phrases as <u>it is</u> or <u>it was</u>.

  EXAMPLE: It was **I** who asked the question.

A. Underline the correct pronoun.

1. It was (I, me) who found the keys.

2. It was (she, her) who lost them.

3. The detectives were (we, us).

4. It was (they, them) who looked in the mailbox.

5. The letter carrier is (she, her).

6. It was (he, him) on the telephone.

7. The speakers were the principal and (I, me).

8. The athlete was (she, her).

9. The photographer was (he, him).

10. That young lady is (she, her).

11. The helper is (he, him).

12. My partners are (they, them).

13. Was it (he, him) who told you?

14. The winner of the race is (she, her).

15. It was (we, us) who were chosen.

16. Was it (I, me) who made the error?

B. Complete these sentences by writing a subject pronoun for the word or words in parentheses.

1. It was _____ who worked out in the gym.   (the school team)

2. The most talented gymnast is _____.   (Susie)

3. Our newest team members are _____.   (Jay and Mark)

4. The coach with the whistle is _____.   (Ms. Parker)

5. The spectators in the gym were _____.   (my parents)

6. The one who is on the parallel bars is _____.   (Bob)

7. The one who is on the balance beam is _____.   (Bill)

8. Our best vaulter is _____.   (Michelle)

9. The athlete on the rings was _____.   (Kristin)

10. The vice-president of the company is _____.   (Mr. Walker)

- Use <u>who</u> as a subject pronoun.   EXAMPLE: **Who** came to the party?
- Use <u>whom</u> as an object pronoun.   EXAMPLE: **Whom** did the nurse help?
- By rearranging the sentence <u>The nurse did help **whom?**,</u> you can see that whom follows the verb and is the object of the verb. It can also be the object of a preposition.   EXAMPLE: To **whom** did you wish to speak?

■ **Complete each sentence with <u>Who</u> or <u>Whom</u>.**

1. _____Who_____ is that man?

2. _____ made the first American flag?

3. _____ would you choose as the winner?

4. _____ is your best friend?

5. _____ gets the reward?

6. _____ will be staying with you at summer camp?

7. _____ did the teacher invite to speak to the class?

8. _____ did you see at the park?

9. _____ will you contact at headquarters?

10. _____ will you write about?

11. _____ is available to baby-sit for me on Saturday?

12. _____ did your mom drive to the dance last Friday?

13. _____ would like to travel to Hawaii next summer?

14. _____ raced in the track meet?

15. _____ did Grandma and Grandpa meet at the airport?

16. _____ are your three favorite authors?

17. _____ owns that new blue bike?

18. _____ did you help last week?

19. _____ wrote that clever poem?

20. _____ will you ask to help you move?

21. _____ brought that salad?

■ **Underline the pronouns in each sentence below.**

1. He went with us to the picnic by the lake.

2. Did you find a magazine in the living room?

3. When are we going to meet at the concert?

4. Are we leaving today?

5. Did you see him?

6. She saw them at the party.

7. He spoke to James and me.

8. Who brought the music for you to play?

9. Mr. and Mrs. Alvarez and I invited them to go to a movie.

10. May brought me these pictures she took.

11. Why can't they go with us?

12. I went with her to get the application form.

13. Louis brought you and him some French coins.

14. Between you and me, I think that last program was silly.

15. Did Miss Tonetti explain the experiment to her and him?

16. Did she find them?

17. May I go with you?

18. He and I sat on the bleachers.

19. They saw me this morning.

20. Who has a library book?

21. For whom shall I ask?

22. I do not have it with me.

23. She told me about the trip to Canada.

24. They are coming to see us.

25. We haven't heard from Uncle James since he left.

26. Come with us.

27. Aren't you and I going with Alan?

28. You should plan the theme before you write it.

29. Aren't they coming for us?

30. Kelly and I gave them a new book of stamps.

31. Steve told us an interesting story about a dog.

32. Who is planning a summer vacation?

33. She and I never expected to see you here!

34. We will visit them this evening.

■ **Underline the correct pronoun.**

1. It was (I, me).

2. Bill and (he, him) are on their way to catch the plane.

3. Nicole and (I, me) have always been good friends.

4. The guard showed (they, them) the entrance to the building.

5. The boss told (I, me) to clean the office.

6. Please take (I, me) to lunch.

7. I am going to wait for (she, her).

8. (Who, Whom) planted those beautiful flowers?

9. Next Saturday Zachary and (I, me) are going fishing.

10. Marie came to see (us, we).

11. To (who, whom) did you send the postcard?

12. This is a secret between you and (I, me).

13. Mrs. Oakley asked Carolyn to move (us, our) table.

14. The committee asked Michael, Kip, and (I, me) to help serve.

15. Did Ellen bring (she, her)?

16. Jamie told (us, we) to get to the station on time.

17. Grant and (she, her) drove the tractors.

18. (Who, Whom) bought this magazine?

19. The boss brought Matt and Kevin (them, their) checks.

20. Martin took Armando and (I, me) to work this morning.

21. With (who, whom) did you play soccer?

22. Michelle painted (she, her) kitchen yesterday.

23. Seven of (us, we) were named to the board of directors.

24. He completed all of (his, him) math problems this morning.

25. (Us, We) are going to play basketball.

26. She called for Janice and (I, me).

27. (Who, Whom) washed the windows?

28. Joyce and (I, me) will fix the broken latch.

29. We came to see (them, they).

30. Will Pamela or (I, me) go with Dad to (him, his) ranch?

31. For (who, whom) are you looking?

32. Did you know it was (her, she)?

33. Lisa and (her, she) are knitting caps.

34. (We, Us) are going to the museum on Saturday.

> - An **adjective** is a word that describes a noun or a pronoun.
>   EXAMPLE: The sky is spotted with **white** clouds.
> - Adjectives usually tell **what kind, which one,** or **how many.**
>   EXAMPLES: **white** roses, **that** mitt, **fifteen** cents

A. Choose an appropriate adjective from the box to describe each noun.

brave	foolish	gorgeous	hasty	shining
cold	fragrant	happy	polite	sly

1. _____ scout

2. _____ flower

3. _____ worker

4. _____ water

5. _____ fox

6. _____ girls

7. _____ sunset

8. _____ dimes

9. _____ prank

10. _____ deeds

B. Write three adjectives that could be used to describe each noun.

1. flowers _____ _____ _____

2. an automobile _____ _____ _____

3. a friend _____ _____ _____

4. a bicycle _____ _____ _____

5. snow _____ _____ _____

6. a baby _____ _____ _____

7. a sunrise _____ _____ _____

8. a book _____ _____ _____

9. a kitten _____ _____ _____

10. a train _____ _____ _____

11. a mountain _____ _____ _____

12. the wind _____ _____ _____

13. a river _____ _____ _____

14. a house _____ _____ _____

- The **articles** a, an, and the are called **limiting adjectives**.
- Use a before words beginning with a consonant sound.
    EXAMPLES: **a** bugle, **a** mountain, **a** sail
- Use an before words beginning with a vowel sound.
    EXAMPLES: **an** oboe, **an** island, **an** anchor

C. Write a or an in each blank.

1.	_____ salesperson		26.	_____ ounce
2.	_____ train		27.	_____ error
3.	_____ newspaper		28.	_____ tablet
4.	_____ iceberg		29.	_____ desk
5.	_____ friend		30.	_____ holiday
6.	_____ election		31.	_____ accident
7.	_____ welder		32.	_____ astronaut
8.	_____ piano		33.	_____ box
9.	_____ game		34.	_____ fire
10.	_____ ant		35.	_____ pilot
11.	_____ eye		36.	_____ mechanic
12.	_____ army		37.	_____ American
13.	_____ telephone		38.	_____ evergreen
14.	_____ orange		39.	_____ aviator
15.	_____ country		40.	_____ hundred
16.	_____ airplane		41.	_____ picture
17.	_____ oak		42.	_____ elephant
18.	_____ engine		43.	_____ letter
19.	_____ ear		44.	_____ umbrella
20.	_____ state		45.	_____ announcer
21.	_____ elm		46.	_____ onion
22.	_____ shoe		47.	_____ umpire
23.	_____ object		48.	_____ car
24.	_____ basket		49.	_____ ice cube
25.	_____ apple		50.	_____ elevator

Proper Adjectives

> ■ A **proper adjective** is an adjective that is formed from a proper noun.
> It always begins with a capital letter.
> EXAMPLES: **Proper Noun**   **Proper Adjective**
> Poland   Polish
> Germany   German
> Paris   Parisian

A. Write a proper adjective formed from each proper noun below. You may wish to check the spelling in a dictionary.

1. South America _____
2. Africa _____
3. England _____
4. Mexico _____
5. France _____
6. Russia _____
7. America _____
8. Rome _____
9. Alaska _____

10. Canada _____
11. Norway _____
12. Scotland _____
13. Ireland _____
14. China _____
15. Spain _____
16. Italy _____
17. Hawaii _____
18. Japan _____

B. Write sentences using proper adjectives you formed in Exercise A.

1.   Many South American countries have warm climates.
2. _____
3. _____
4. _____
5. _____
6. _____
7. _____
8. _____
9. _____
10. _____

Demonstrative Adjectives

- A **demonstrative adjective** is an adjective that points out a specific person or thing.
- This and that describe singular nouns. This points to a person or thing nearby, and that points to a person or thing farther away.
   EXAMPLES: **This** room is my favorite. **That** boy is running very fast.
- These and those describe plural nouns. These points to persons or things nearby, and those points to persons or things farther away.
   EXAMPLES: **These** girls are the best players. **Those** houses need painting.
- The word them is a pronoun. Never use it to describe a noun.

A. Underline the correct demonstrative adjective.

1. Please hand me (those, this) red candles.

2. Where did you buy (these, that) large pecans?

3. Did you grow (these, them) roses in your garden?

4. Please bring me (those, that) wrench.

5. Where did Marc find (these, this) watermelon?

6. (Those, Them) glasses belong to Mike.

7. Do you want one of (these, this) calendars?

8. May I use one of (these, them) pencils?

9. Did you see (those, them) films of Africa?

10. Calvin, where are (those, that) people going?

11. Did you see (those, them) police officers?

12. Please put (those, this) books in the box.

13. (That, Those) floor needs to be cleaned.

14. Sarah and Joe might buy (those, that) car.

15. (That, These) cabinets will be repainted.

16. Please close (that, those) door.

17. Will you fix the flat tire on (this, these) bike?

18. (This, Those) letter needs a stamp before you mail it.

B. Write four sentences using this, that, these, or those.

1. _____

2. _____

3. _____

4. _____

> ■ An adjective has three degrees of comparison: **positive**, **comparative**, and **superlative.**
> ■ The simple form of the adjective is called the **positive** degree.
>   EXAMPLE: Anita is **tall.**
> ■ When two people or things are being compared, the **comparative** degree is used.
>   EXAMPLE: Anita is **taller** than Nancy.
> ■ When three or more people or things are being compared, the **superlative** degree is used.
>   EXAMPLE: Anita is the **tallest** girl in the group.
> ■ For all adjectives of one syllable and a few adjectives of two syllables, add -er to form the comparative degree and -est to form the superlative degree.
>   EXAMPLE: rich — richer — richest
> ■ If the adjective ends in -y, change the -y to -i and add -er or -est.
>   EXAMPLE: tiny — tinier — tiniest

■ **Write the comparative and superlative forms.**

POSITIVE	COMPARATIVE	SUPERLATIVE
1. smooth		
2. young		
3. sweet		
4. strong		
5. lazy		
6. great		
7. kind		
8. calm		
9. rough		
10. narrow		
11. deep		
12. short		
13. happy		
14. cold		
15. pretty		

- For some adjectives of two syllables and all adjectives of three or more syllables, use more to form the comparative and most to form the superlative.
  - EXAMPLES: He thinks that the lily is **more** fragrant than the tulip.
  - He thinks that the carnation is the **most** fragrant flower of all.
- Comparison of adjectives also can be used to indicate less or least of a quality. Use less to form the comparative and least to form the superlative.
  - EXAMPLES: I see Josie **less** often than I see Terry.
  - I see Josh **least** often of all.
- Some adjectives have irregular comparisons.
  - EXAMPLES: good, better, best   bad, worse, worst

A. Write the comparative and superlative forms using more and most.

POSITIVE	COMPARATIVE	SUPERLATIVE
1. energetic	_____	_____
2. courteous	_____	_____
3. impatient	_____	_____
4. important	_____	_____
5. difficult	_____	_____
6. wonderful	_____	_____
7. gracious	_____	_____
8. agreeable	_____	_____

B. Write the comparative and superlative forms using less and least.

POSITIVE	COMPARATIVE	SUPERLATIVE
1. helpful	_____	_____
2. friendly	_____	_____
3. serious	_____	_____
4. agreeable	_____	_____
5. faithful	_____	_____
6. comfortable	_____	_____
7. patient	_____	_____
8. reliable	_____	_____

C. Write the correct degree of comparison for the adjective in parentheses.

1. (near)   Which planet is _____ the earth, Venus or Jupiter?

2. (tall)   Who is the _____ of the three brothers?

3. (helpful)   Who is _____, Sandra or Linda?

4. (young)   Who is _____, Sandra or Linda?

5. (difficult)   I think this is the _____ problem in the lesson.

6. (good)   Is "A Ghost Story" a _____ story than "The Last Leaf"?

7. (small)   What is our _____ state?

8. (hot)   In our state, August is usually the _____ month.

9. (young)   Hans is the _____ person at the factory.

10. (wide)   The Amazon is the _____ river in the world.

11. (old)   Who is _____, David or Steve?

12. (large)   What is the _____ city in your state?

13. (courteous)   Dan is always the _____ person at a party.

14. (good)   This poem is the _____ one I have read this year.

15. (cold)   This must be the _____ night so far this winter.

16. (studious)   Of the two sisters, Andrea is the _____.

17. (tall)   Who is _____, Kay or Carol?

18. (wealthy)   This is the home of the _____ banker in our city.

19. (fast)   Who is the _____ worker in the office?

20. (useful)   Which is _____, electric lights or the telephone?

21. (beautiful)   Your garden is the _____ one I have seen.

22. (narrow)   That is the _____ of all the bridges on the road.

23. (large)   Cleveland is _____ than Cincinnati.

24. (good)   Of the three books, this one is the _____.

25. (bad)   That is the _____ collection in the museum.

26. (famous)   Washington became the _____ general of the Revolution.

27. (beautiful)   I think tulips are the _____ kind of flower.

> ■ An **adverb** is a word that describes a verb, an adjective, or another adverb.
> EXAMPLES: The parade moved **slowly.** Your tie is **very** colorful.
> You did this **too** quickly.
> ■ An adverb usually tells **how, when, where,** or **how often.**
> ■ Many adverbs end in -ly.

A. Write two adverbs that could be used to describe each verb.

1. laugh _____

_____

2. talk _____

_____

3. stand _____

_____

4. sing _____

_____

5. swim _____

_____

6. eat _____

_____

7. read _____

_____

8. work _____

_____

9. write _____

_____

10. walk _____

_____

11. jump _____

_____

12. move _____

_____

13. run _____

_____

14. speak _____

_____

15. listen _____

_____

16. drive _____

_____

17. sit _____

_____

18. dance _____

_____

B. Use each adverb in a sentence.

well	regularly	early
softly	very	here

1. _____

2. _____

3. _____

4. _____

5. _____

6. _____

C. Underline the adverb or adverbs in each sentence.

1. The old car moved slowly up the hill.

2. She answered him very quickly.

3. We arrived at the party too early, so we helped with the decorations.

4. The family waited patiently to hear about the newborn baby.

5. Cindy drove the car very cautiously in the snowstorm.

6. Does Marshall always sit here, or may I have this seat?

7. They walked very rapidly in order to get home before the rainstorm.

8. The dog ran swiftly toward its home.

9. Emily quietly waited her turn while others went ahead.

10. These oaks grow very slowly, but they are worth the long wait.

11. May I speak now, or should I wait for his call?

12. We searched everywhere for the inflatable rafts and life preservers.

13. The nights have been extremely warm, so we go swimming every evening.

14. He always speaks distinctly and practices good manners.

15. Can you swim far underwater without coming up for air?

16. Come here, and I'll show you ladybugs in the grass.

17. Please answer quickly so hat we can finish before recess.

18. Deer run very fast, especially at the first sign of danger.

19. I suddenly remembered that I left my jacket in the park.

20. The snow fell softly on the rooftops of the mountain village.

21. I can pack our lunches and be there by noon.

22. She wrote too rapidly and made a mistake.

23. Winters there are extremely cold, but summers are very pleasant.

24. The pianist bowed politely to the audience.

25. You are reading too rapidly to learn something from it.

26. The team played extremely well.

27. The cat walked softly toward a fly on the windowpane.

28. Everyone listened carefully to the sound of a bluebird singing.

29. We walked wearily toward the bus in the hot sun.

30. We crossed the street very carefully at the beginning of the parade.

31. We eagerly watched the game from the rooftop deck of our building.

32. The recreation center was finished recently.

33. We walked everywhere yesterday.

34. My grandmother dearly loves her red hat.

35. I have read this book before.

36. He wants badly to learn to play the guitar.

- An **adverb** has three degrees of comparison: **positive, comparative,** and **superlative.**
- The simple form of the adverb is called the **positive** degree.
    EXAMPLE: Joe worked **hard** to complete the job.
- When two actions are being compared, the **comparative** degree is used.
    EXAMPLE: Joe worked **harder** than Jim.
- When three or more actions are being compared, the **superlative** degree is used.
    EXAMPLE: Tony worked **hardest** of all.
- Use -er to form the comparative degree and use -est to form the superlative degree of one-syllable adverbs.
- Use more or most with longer adverbs and with adverbs that end in -ly.
    EXAMPLE: Jan danced **more** gracefully than Tania.
    Vicki danced the **most** gracefully of all the students.

- **Complete each sentence using the comparative or superlative form of the underlined adverb.**

1. David can jump <u>high</u>. Diane can jump _____ than David.

    Donna can jump the _____ of all.

2. Grant arrives <u>late</u> for the party. Gina arrives _____

    than Grant. Gail arrives _____ of anyone.

3. Dawn walks <u>slowly</u> in the park. Tomás walks _____

    than Dawn. Sam walks _____ of all.

4. Jean spoke <u>clearly</u> before the class. Jon spoke _____

    than Jean. Joseph spoke _____ of all the students.

5. Alex scrubbed <u>hard</u>. Anne scrubbed _____ than Alex.

    Alice scrubbed the _____ of all.

6. You can lose weight <u>quickly</u> by running. A nutritious diet works _____

    than just running. Of all weight-loss programs, combining the two works

    _____.

7. Tania played the flute <u>beautifully</u>. Tara played the clarinet even _____.

    Rick played the oboe the _____ of them all.

8. Chrissy has been waiting <u>long</u>. Mr. Norris has been waiting even _____.

    Justin has been waiting the _____ of all.

- <u>Doesn't</u> is the contraction of <u>does not</u>. Use it with singular nouns and the pronouns <u>he</u>, <u>she</u>, and <u>it</u>.
  EXAMPLES: The dog **doesn't** want to play. She **doesn't** want to go.
- <u>Don't</u> is the contraction of <u>do not</u>. Use it with plural nouns and the pronouns <u>I</u>, <u>you</u>, <u>we</u>, and <u>they</u>.
  EXAMPLES: The children **don't** have their books. We **don't** have time.

■ **Underline the correct contraction to complete each sentence.**

1. I (doesn't, don't) know why he (doesn't, don't) like that movie star.

2. Why (doesn't, don't) the caretaker open the gates earlier?

3. (Doesn't, Don't) your sister coach the team, Tom?

4. (Doesn't, Don't) this office need more fresh air?

5. (Doesn't, Don't) this sweater belong to you, Katie?

6. We (doesn't, don't) go home at noon for lunch.

7. (Doesn't, Don't) your sister attend the state university?

8. The child (doesn't, don't) want to miss the parade.

9. Angelo (doesn't, don't) like to play tennis.

10. It (doesn't, don't) take long to learn to swim.

11. Some of the elevators (doesn't, don't) go to the top floor.

12. Eric (doesn't, don't) know how to ride a bicycle.

13. He (doesn't, don't) know that we are here.

14. We (doesn't, don't) listen to our radio often.

15. Why (doesn't, don't) Craig get here on time?

16. This problem (doesn't, don't) seem difficult to me.

17. (Doesn't, Don't) it look hot outside?

18. Why (doesn't, don't) Paul go, too?

19. She (doesn't, don't) want to go to the movie.

20. Kelly (doesn't, don't) have that written in her notebook.

21. (Doesn't, Don't) you want to go with us?

22. Why (doesn't, don't) your friend come to our meetings?

23. Neil Brown (doesn't, don't) go to night school.

24. Melissa (doesn't, don't) eat ice cream.

25. Jody and Ray (doesn't, don't) like science fiction movies.

26. The people (doesn't, don't) have to wait outside.

27. (Doesn't, Don't) you want to come with us?

28. They (doesn't, don't) know if it will rain today.

> ■ Use <u>may</u> to ask for permission.
>   EXAMPLE: **May** I go with you?
> ■ Use <u>can</u> to express the ability to do something.
>   EXAMPLE: James **can** swim well.

A. Complete each sentence with <u>may</u> or <u>can</u>.

1. Adam, _____ you whistle?

2. His dog _____ do three difficult tricks.

3. Miss Nance, _____ I leave work early?

4. I _____ see the airplane in the distance.

5. Chris, _____ you tie a good knot?

6. Carlos, _____ I drive your car?

7. You _____ see the mountains from here.

8. My grandmother _____ drive us home.

9. The Garcias _____ speak three languages.

10. _____ I examine those new books?

> ■ <u>Teach</u> means "to give instruction."
>   EXAMPLE: I'll **teach** you how to shoot free throws.
> ■ <u>Learn</u> means "to acquire knowledge."
>   EXAMPLE: When did you **learn** to speak Spanish?

B. Complete each sentence with <u>teach</u> or <u>learn</u>.

1. I think he will _____ me quickly.

2. I will _____ to recite that poem.

3. Did your parents _____ you to build a fire?

4. The women are going to _____ to use the new machines.

5. Will you _____ me to play tennis?

6. My brother is going to _____ Billy to skate.

7. Would you like to _____ the rules of the game to them?

8. No one can _____ you if you do not try to _____.

Using *Sit/Set* and *Lay/Lie*

> - Sit means "to take a resting position." Its principal parts are <u>sit</u>, <u>sitting</u>, and <u>sat</u>.
>   EXAMPLES: Please **sit** here. He **sat** beside her.
> - Set means "to place." Its principal parts are <u>set</u>, <u>setting</u>, and <u>set</u>.
>   EXAMPLES: Will you please **set** this dish on the table?
>   She **set** the table for dinner last night.

A. Underline the correct verb.

1. Please (sit, set) down, Kathleen.

2. Where should we (sit, set) the television?

3. Where do you (sit, set)?

4. Pamela, please (sit, set) those plants out this afternoon.

5. (Sit, Set) the basket of groceries on the patio.

6. Mr. Romero usually (sits, sets) on this side of the table.

7. Please come and (sit, set) your books down on that desk.

8. Have you ever (sat, set) by this window?

9. Does he (sit, set) in this seat?

10. Why don't you (sit, set) over here?

> - Lie means "to recline" or "to occupy a certain space." Its principal parts
>   are <u>lie</u>, <u>lying</u>, <u>lay</u>, and <u>lain</u>.
>   EXAMPLES: Why don't you **lie** down for a while?
>   He **has lain** in the hammock all afternoon.
> - Lay means "to place." Its principal parts are <u>lay</u>, <u>laying</u>, <u>laid</u>, and <u>lain</u>.
>   EXAMPLES: The men **are laying** new carpeting in the house.
>   Who **laid** the wet towel on the table?

B. Underline the correct verb.

1. Where did you (lie, lay) your gloves, Betsy?

2. (Lie, Lay) down, Spot.

3. He always (lies, lays) down to rest when he is very tired.

4. Where have you (lain, laid) the evening paper?

5. Please (lie, lay) this box on the desk.

6. Do not (lie, lay) on that dusty hay.

7. (Lay, Lie) the papers on top of the desk.

8. I (laid, lain) the shovel on that pile of dirt.

9. I need to (lie, lay) down to rest.

10. She has (laid, lain) on the sofa all morning.

■ A **preposition** is a word that shows the relationship of a noun or a pronoun to another word in the sentence.
  EXAMPLES: Put the package **on** the table. Place the package **in** the desk.
■ These are some commonly used prepositions:

about	against	at	between	from	of	through	under
above	among	behind	by	in	on	to	upon
across	around	beside	for	into	over	toward	with

■ **Draw a line under each preposition or prepositions in the sentences below.**

1. The grin on Juan's face was bright and warm.

2. He greeted his cousin from Brazil with a smile and a handshake.

3. They walked through the airport and toward the baggage area.

4. Juan found his bags between two boxes.

5. The two cousins had not seen each other for five years.

6. They could spend hours talking about everything.

7. Juan and Luis got into Juan's truck.

8. Juan drove Luis to Juan's family's ranch.

9. It was a long ride across many hills and fields.

10. Luis rested his head against the seat.

11. Soon they drove over a hill and into a valley.

12. The ranch was located across the Harrison River.

13. The house stood among a group of oak trees.

14. Juan parked the truck beside the driveway.

15. They walked across the driveway and toward the house.

16. Juan's mother, Anita, stood behind the screen door.

17. Juan's family gathered around Luis.

18. Everyone sat on the porch and drank lemonade.

19. "Tell us about our relatives in Brazil," Rosa asked.

20. "You have over twenty cousins in my area," said Luis.

21. They go to school, just like you do.

22. Then everyone went into the house and ate dinner.

23. Juan's family passed the food across the table.

24. "Many of these dishes come from old family recipes," he said.

25. "It is wonderful to be among so many relatives," Luis said.

26. After dinner, everyone went to the living room.

27. Luis showed them photographs of his home in Brazil.

> - A **prepositional phrase** is a group of words that begins with a preposition and ends with a noun or pronoun. EXAMPLE: Count the books **on the shelf.**
> - The noun or pronoun in a prepositional phrase is called the **object of the preposition.** EXAMPLE: Count the books on the **shelf.**

■ **Put parentheses around each prepositional phrase. Then underline each preposition, and circle the object of the preposition.**

1. The founders (of our country) had a vision (of a great America).

2. We climbed into the station wagon.

3. Many stars can be seen on a clear night.

4. The top of my desk has been varnished.

5. Have you ever gone through a tunnel?

6. Place these memos on the bulletin board.

7. We have a display of posters in the showcase in the corridor.

8. Carol, take these reports to Mrs. Garza.

9. What is the capital of Alabama?

10. The fabric on this antique sofa came from France.

11. Are you a collector of minerals?

12. I am going to Julia's house.

13. The hillside was dotted with beautiful wild flowers.

14. The rain beat against the windowpanes.

15. We placed a horseshoe above the door.

16. This poem was written by my oldest sister.

17. Great clusters of grapes hung from the vine.

18. Is he going to the race?

19. A herd of goats grazed on the hillside.

20. Are you carrying those books to the storeroom?

21. Our car stalled on the bridge.

22. My grandfather lives in St. Louis.

23. A small vase of flowers was placed in the center of the table.

24. The group sat around the fireplace.

25. The cold wind blew from the north.

26. Doris hit the ball over the fence.

27. The dog played with the bone.

28. High weeds grow by the narrow path.

■ A prepositional phrase can be used to describe a noun or a pronoun. Then the prepositional phrase is being used as an **adjective** to tell which one, what kind, or how many.
EXAMPLE: The chair **in the corner** needs to be repaired.
The prepositional phrase in the corner tells **which** chair.

■ A prepositional phrase can be used to describe a verb. Then the prepositional phrase is being used as an **adverb** to tell how, where, or when.
EXAMPLE: Mrs. Porter repaired the chair **during the evening.**
The prepositional phrase during the evening tells **when** Mrs. Porter repaired the chair.

■ **Underline the prepositional phrase in each sentence. Write adjective or adverb to tell how the phrase is used.**

1. Molly went to the library. _____

2. She needed a book about cooking. _____

3. The shelves in the library contained many books. _____

4. She asked the librarian with blue shoes. _____

5. The librarian in the green dress was very helpful. _____

6. She taught Molly about the card catalog. _____

7. The card catalog has a card for every book. _____

8. The cards are organized in alphabetical order. _____

9. Some cookbooks were in the sports section. _____

10. Molly's trip to the library was a great success. _____

11. The students in seventh grade are having a contest. _____

12. Each student in the class takes a spelling test. _____

13. The tests are given on Friday. _____

14. The number of correctly spelled words is posted. _____

15. A winner is selected for each month. _____

16. The winner of the prize chooses the next words. _____

17. The chosen words must be spelled by the students. _____

18. The teacher brings an apple for the winner. _____

Conjunctions

> ■ A **conjunction** is a word used to join words or groups of words.
>   EXAMPLES: Sally **and** Barb worked late. We worked **until** he arrived.
> ■ These are some commonly used conjunctions:
>
> | although | because | however | or | that | until | whether |
> | and | but | if | since | though | when | while |
> | as | for | nor | than | unless | whereas | yet |
>
> ■ Some conjunctions are used in pairs. These include either . . . or, neither . . . nor, and not only . . . but also.

A. Underline each conjunction in the sentences below.

1. We waited until the mechanic replaced the part.

2. Plums and peaches are my favorite fruits.

3. The wind blew, and the rain fell.

4. Please call Alan or Grant for me.

5. A conjunction may connect words or groups of words.

6. Cotton and wheat are grown on nearby farms.

7. Neither Ann nor Bonnie is my cousin.

8. Their home is not large, but it is comfortable.

9. Father and Sue arrived on time.

10. Do not move the vase, for you may drop it.

B. Complete each sentence with a conjunction.

1. I cannot leave _____ the baby-sitter arrives.

2. We must hurry, _____ we'll be late for work.

3. Battles were fought on the sea, on the land, _____ in the air.

4. Charles _____ Ricky went to the movie, _____ Donald did not.

5. Please wait _____ Elizabeth gets ready.

6. Rolando _____ I will carry that box upstairs.

7. Peter _____ Danny are twins.

8. We will stay home _____ you cannot go.

9. This nation exports cotton _____ wheat.

10. _____ the girls _____ the boys wanted to take another test.

- An **interjection** is a word or group of words that expresses emotion.
  EXAMPLE: **Hurrah!** Our team has won the game.
- If the interjection is used to express sudden or strong feeling, it is followed by an exclamation mark.
  EXAMPLE: **Wow!** You've really done it this time.
- If the interjection is used to express mild emotion, it is followed by a comma.
  EXAMPLE: **Oh,** I see what you mean.
- These are some commonly used interjections:

ah	good grief	oh	ugh
aha	gosh	oops	well
alas	hurrah	sh	whew

- **Write sentences with the following interjections.**

1. Ah _____

2. Wow _____

3. Oh _____

4. Ugh _____

5. Ouch _____

6. Oops _____

7. Hurrah _____

8. Oh no _____

9. Gosh _____

10. Sh _____

11. Help _____

12. Well _____

13. Whew _____

14. Indeed _____

15. Hush _____

16. Goodness _____

17. Aha _____

18. Ha _____

A. Underline the correct verb or the correct pronoun.

1. Have you (saw, seen) Matthew this morning?

2. Mom (did, done) all of the driving.

3. Maria (came, come) home a few minutes ago.

4. I (took, taken) my bicycle to the shop last Saturday.

5. Where has your teacher (went, gone)?

6. I haven't (wrote, written) my invitations yet.

7. Gina (gave, given) her book report yesterday.

8. It (don't, doesn't) take much time to walk to school.

9. Where (was, were) you going after school yesterday?

10. Mark will go with Pam and (I, me) to visit Grandma.

11. Beth and (I, me) signed up for music lessons.

12. Please take (we, us) with you when you go to the mall.

13. (They, Them) wanted to watch the Olympic Games on television.

14. (He, Him) was worried about finishing the test on time.

15. Give (they, them) those books and boxes.

B. Complete each sentence with the possessive form of the word in parentheses.

1. (mother) The _____ group held a book sale at school.

2. (children) The _____ classes came at different times.

3. (teachers) All of our _____ favorite books were there.

4. (singers) The _____ voices blended perfectly together.

C. Underline each adjective. Circle each adverb.

1. This small coat fit comfortably last year.

2. The large basket was filled with pink roses.

3. Many mistakes are caused by carelessness.

4. The fastest runners ran easily to the finish line.

D. Put parentheses around each prepositional phrase. Then underline each preposition and circle the object of the preposition.

1. Put this basket of clothes in the laundry room.

2. The hillside was covered with yellow daisies.

3. The top of the mountain is usually covered with snow.

4. The house on the corner was sold in one week.

Using What You've Learned

A. Read the following paragraphs.

      Christopher Columbus was born in the city of Genoa, Italy, around 1451. His father, a weaver, made cloth. Columbus learned many sailing skills because he grew up close to the sea. He worked on an Italian merchant ship and was shipwrecked on the rocky coast of Portugal. While he was in Portugal, he quickly learned new ways to build ships and to navigate. Columbus made several voyages along the African coast and even traveled as far north as Iceland.

      Columbus first suggested the idea of sailing west to find a route to Japan and China to King John II of Portugal. The king was not interested, so Columbus went to the rulers of Spain, King Ferdinand and Queen Isabella. In 1492, the king and queen wisely granted their permission to Columbus and gave him three ships: the *Niña,* the *Pinta,* and the *Santa Maria.* Columbus set sail with a crew of ninety men.

B. In the paragraphs, find six common nouns, and write them on the lines below. Circle those that are plural.

1. _____   3. _____   5. _____

2. _____   4. _____   6. _____

C. Find six proper nouns, and write them on the lines below.

1. _____   3. _____   5. _____

2. _____   4. _____   6. _____

D. Find two proper adjectives and the nouns they describe, and write them on the lines below.

1. _____   2. _____

E. Find two adverbs and the verbs they describe, and write them on the lines below.

1. _____   2. _____

F. Find a sentence with an appositive, and write the sentence on the lines below.

_____

_____

G. Find six prepositional phrases, and write them on the lines below.

1. _____   4. _____

2. _____   5. _____

3. _____   6. _____

H. Rewrite the following paragraphs. Correct any mistakes in the use of nouns, pronouns, or verbs.

In 1585, a group of about 100 men come from England to Roanoke Island to sit up a colony. Them did not have enough food or supply's. The Indians was unfriendly. The group chosen to abandon the colony. In 1586, Sir Francis Drakes fleet stopped at the colony and took the men back to England.

The English people would not give up. In 1587, three ship left England. A group of 117 men, woman, and childrens settled on Roanoke Island. They expected to live on the supplies them received from England. In 1590, when the supply ships arriving in Roanoke, the colonists who had came in 1587 had disappeared. The people of Roanoke was never found. Their disappearance is a mysteries that has never been solved.

_____

_____

_____

_____

_____

_____

_____

_____

_____

_____

_____

_____

_____

_____

_____

_____

_____

- ■ **Capitalize** the first word of a sentence.
    - EXAMPLE: Let's take a walk to the park.
- ■ Capitalize the first word of a quotation.
    - EXAMPLE: Lenny said, "It's time for lunch."

A. Circle each letter that should be capitalized. Write the capital letter above it.

1. haven't you made an appointment to meet them?

2. the twins will go to the game together.

3. danielle asked, "how did she like the book?"

4. the family moved to another state last year.

5. "bring your scripts to the practice," said the director.

6. who wrote this article for the school newspaper?

7. the little girl said, "my party is in one week."

8. "have some more carrot sticks," said the host.

- ■ Capitalize the first word of every line of poetry.
    - EXAMPLE: The strong winds whipped
      - The sails of the ship
- ■ Capitalize the first, last, and all important words in the titles of books, poems, songs, and stories.
    - EXAMPLES: *Gone with the Wind*   "America the Beautiful"

B. Circle each letter that should be capitalized. Write the capital letter above it.

1. i eat my peas with honey;

   i've done it all my life.

   it makes the peas taste funny,

   but it keeps them on the knife!

2. it's midnight, and the setting sun

   is slowly rising in the west;

   the rapid rivers slowly run,

   the frog is on his downy nest.

3. Who wrote the poem "the children's hour"?

4. My favorite novel is *a wrinkle in time.*

5. The sixth-grade band played "stand by me."

6. During the summer, Kim read *adam of the road.*

7. Carla gave her poem the title "chasing the wind."

> - Capitalize all **proper nouns.**
>   EXAMPLES: Sarah, Dad, Arbor Street, England, Maine, Arctic Ocean,
>   Ural Mountains, Columbus Day, February, Academy School, *Ocean Queen*
> - Capitalize all **proper adjectives.** A proper adjective is an adjective that
>   is made from a proper noun.
>   EXAMPLES: the Spanish language, American food, Chinese people

C. Rewrite the following paragraph. Be sure to add capital letters where they are needed.

chris and her friends went to a festival in chicago. Some of them tasted greek pastry and canadian cheese soup. charley thought that the italian sausage and mexican tacos were delicious! laurel tried an unusual japanese salad. They all watched some irish folk dancers and listened to german music.

_____

_____

_____

_____

_____

_____

_____

_____

D. Circle each letter that should be capitalized. Write the capital letter above it.

1. Did anita and her family drive through arizona, new mexico, and colorado?

2. Isn't brazil larger in area than the united states?

3. Did mark twain live in the small town of hannibal, missouri?

4. Have you read the story of martin luther king?

5. I have been reading about the solomon islands.

6. The north sea is connected with the english channel by the strait of dover.

7. At thirteen, sam houston moved to tennessee from lexington, virginia.

8. Isn't st. augustine the oldest city in the united states?

9. Is albany the capital of new york?

10. Our teacher brought japanese money back from her trip.

> ■ Capitalize a person's title when it comes before a name.
>   EXAMPLES: Doctor Baker, Governor Alvarez, Senator Washington
> ■ Capitalize abbreviations of titles.
>   EXAMPLES: Dr. Garcia, Supt. Barbara Shurna, Mr. J. Howell, Sr.

E. Circle each letter that should be capitalized. Write the capital letter above it.

1. Did captain cheng congratulate sergeant walters on his promotion?

2. The new health plan was developed by dr. ruth banks and mr. juan gomez.

3. After an introduction, pres. alice slater presented the next speaker, mr. allen norman.

4. When did principal grissom invite mayor hadley to attend the graduation ceremony?

5. Officer halpern was the first to stand up when judge patterson entered the courtroom.

6. How long has mrs. frank been working for president howell?

7. Does prof. mary schneider teach this course, or does dr. david towne?

8. Prince andrew of england will tour the southern states in the fall.

9. Senator alan howell is the uncle of supt. joyce randall.

> ■ Capitalize abbreviations of days and months, parts of addresses, and
>   titles of members of the armed forces. Also capitalize all letters in
>   abbreviations for states.
>   EXAMPLES: Fri., Jan., 3720 E. Franklin Ave., Gen. H. J. Farrimond,
>   Los Angeles, CA, Dallas, TX

F. Circle each letter that should be capitalized. Write the capital letter above it.

1. capt. margaret k. hansen

   2075 lakeview st.

   phoenix, az 85072

2. jackson school Track Meet

   at wilson stadium

   tues., sept. 26, 10:30

   649 n. clark blvd.

3. mr. harold bernt

   4938 s. vernon ave.

   chicago, il 60637

4. lt. gary l. louis

   5931 congress rd.

   syracuse, ny 13217

5. thanksgiving Concert

   wed., nov. 23, 11:00

   Practice tues., nov. 22, 3:30

   See ms. evans for details.

6. gen. david grimes

   329 n. hayes st.

   louisville, ky 40227

> ■ Use a **period** at the end of a declarative sentence.
>   EXAMPLE: Theresa's aunt lives in Florida.
> ■ Use a **question mark** at the end of an interrogative sentence.
>   EXAMPLE: Will you carry this package for me?

A. Use a period or question mark to end each sentence below.

1. Mrs. Clark has moved her law office____

2. Isn't this Dorothy's baseball glove____

3. Are you moving to Massachusetts next month____

4. It's too late to buy tickets for the game____

5. Our program will begin in five minutes____

6. Does your sister drive a truck____

7. Ms. Tobin's store was damaged by the flood____

8. Are you going to Rebecca's birthday party____

9. Lucy did not take the plane to St. Petersburg____

10. Do you have a stamp for this envelope____

11. Have you ever seen Clarence laugh so hard____

12. President Sophia Harris called the meeting to order____

13. Will Gilmore Plumbing be open on Labor Day____

14. School ends the second week in June____

15. We are going camping in Canada this summer____

B. Add the correct end punctuation where needed in the paragraph below.

Have you ever been to the Olympic Games____ If not, have you ever seen them on television____ I hope to see them in person some day____ The Olympic Games are held every four years in a different country____ The games started in ancient Greece, but the games as we now know them date back to 1896____ Some of the finest athletes in the world compete for bronze, silver, and gold medals____ Can you think of a famous Olympic athlete____ What is your favorite Olympic sport____ It could be a winter or summer sport because the games are held for each season____ One American athlete won seven gold medals in swimming____ Can you imagine how excited that athlete must have felt, knowing that he had represented America so well____ That is the American record to date____ However, there will be plenty more chances for that record to be broken____

> - Use a period at the end of an imperative sentence.
>   EXAMPLE: Close the door to the attic.
> - Use an **exclamation point** at the end of an exclamatory sentence and after an interjection that shows strong feelings.
>   EXAMPLES: What a great shot! I'd love to go with you! Wow!

C. Add periods and exclamation points where needed in the sentences below.

1. Address the envelope to Dr. George K. Zimmerman____

2. How nicely dressed you are____

3. Hurry____ The bus is ready to leave____

4. Get some paints for your next art lesson____

5. Shake hands with Mr. D. B. Norton____

6. Oops____ I spilled the glass of orange juice____

7. Carry this bag to the car in the parking lot____

8. What a great view you have from your apartment window____

9. Wipe the counter when you're through eating____

10. Oh, what a beautiful painting____

11. I can't wait until summer vacation____

12. Please take this to the post office for me____

13. Just look at the size of the fish he caught____

14. I've never seen a larger one____

15. Get the net from under the life preserver____

16. I sure hope the pictures come out well____

D. Add the correct end punctuation where needed in the paragraph below.

The state of Maine in New England is a wonderful place to visit in the summer or winter____ Have you ever been there____ It is best known for its rocky coastline on the Atlantic Ocean____ Visitors often drive along the rugged coast____ There are numerous quaint sea towns along the coast that date back to the 1600s____ What a long time ago that was____ Mount Katahdin and the northern part of the Appalachian Mountains are ideal places for winter sports, such as downhill and cross-country skiing____ If you've never seen a deer or moose, you'd probably see plenty of them while hiking in Acadia National Park____ It has over 30,000 acres____ Do you know anything about Maine's local fish____ Well, there are many kinds that are native to its rivers and lakes____ But Maine is famous for its Atlantic lobsters____ Rockport and Rockland are two of the largest cities for lobster fishing____ Lobsters from northern Maine are flown all over the world____ Blueberries are another big product of Maine____ Have you ever had wild blueberries____ Some people consider them to be the best____

> ■ Use a **comma** between words or groups of words in a series.
>   EXAMPLE: Be sure your business letter is brief, courteous, and correct.
> ■ Use a comma before a conjunction in a compound sentence.
>   EXAMPLE: Neal sketched the cartoon, and Clare wrote the caption.

A. Add commas where needed in the sentences below.

1. We export cotton corn and wheat to many countries.

2. The children played softball ran races and pitched horseshoes.

3. Lauren held the nail and Tasha hit it with a hammer.

4. Alice Henry Carmen and James go to the library often.

5. The pitcher threw a fastball and the batter struck out.

6. Sara peeled the peaches and Victor sliced them.

7. The mountains were covered with forests of pine cedar and oak.

8. Craig should stop running or he will be out of breath.

9. Baseball is Lee's favorite sport but Sue's favorite is football.

10. Limestone marble granite and slate are found in Vermont New Hampshire and Maine.

11. The rain fell steadily and the lightning flashed.

12. Mindy enjoyed the corn but Frank preferred the string beans.

> ■ Use a comma to set off a quotation from the rest of a sentence.
>   EXAMPLES: "We must get up early," said Mom.
>   Mom said, "We must get up early."

B. Add commas before or after the quotations below.

1. "Please show me how this machine works" said Carolyn.

2. "Be sure you keep your eyes on the road" said the driving instructor.

3. Rick replied "I can't believe my ears."

4. Gail said "Travel is dangerous on the icy roads."

5. "Paul studied piano for two years" said Ms. Walters.

6. Alex said "That goat eats everything in sight."

7. "Let's go to the park for a picnic" said Marie.

8. "Wait for me here" said Paul.

9. Tom said "Grandmother, thank you for the present."

10. "I'm going to the game with Al" remarked Frank.

11. Al asked "What time should we leave?"

12. Chris remembered "I was only five when we moved to New York."

- Use a comma to set off the name of a person who is being addressed.
  EXAMPLE: Betty, did you find the answer to your question?
- Use a comma to set off words like yes, no, well, and oh at the beginning of a sentence.
  EXAMPLE: No, I haven't seen Jack today.
- Use a comma to set off an appositive.
  EXAMPLE: Jack, Mary's brother, is going to college next fall.

C. Add commas where needed in the sentences below.

1. Miss Hunt do you know the answer to that question?

2. Can't you find the book I brought you last week Roger?

3. Dr. Levin the Smith's dentist sees patients on weekends.

4. Oh I guess it takes about an hour to get to Denver.

5. Dad may Sam and I go to the ball game?

6. Our neighbor Billy Johnson is a carpenter.

7. What is the population of your state Linda?

8. Well I'm not sure of the exact number.

9. Beth are you going skiing this weekend?

10. What time are you going to the concert Greg?

11. Our teacher Mr. St. James also coaches the softball team.

12. Sue have you seen a small black cat around your neighborhood?

13. Jeff do you know Mr. D. B. Norton?

14. No I don't think we've ever met.

15. Sally and John would you like to go shopping on Saturday?

16. Mrs. Porter our principal is retiring this year.

17. Yes the teachers are planning a retirement dinner for her.

18. Mrs. Porter and her husband Dr. Hal Porter plan to move to Oregon.

D. Add commas where needed in the paragraph below.

Margie Carol and I are going to Sunset Pines a summer camp in Michigan. None of us has ever been to camp before but we are looking forward to it. "Will you bring your swimsuit goggles and fins?" Carol asked us. "Oh Carol that's a great idea" I replied. Margie my favorite cousin suggested that we make lists of what to pack and compare our lists. Margie said "Let's not forget to pack paper stamps and envelopes so we can write to our families." Carol said "We have plenty of room in our suitcases but let's not bring things we won't use." I added "Of course we will not want to leave behind certain things like snacks bug spray and a radio!"

> - Use **quotation marks** to show the exact words of a speaker. Use a comma or another punctuation mark to separate the quotation from the rest of the sentence.
>   EXAMPLES: "Do you have a book on helicopters?" asked Tom.
>   James said, "It's right here."
> - A quotation may be placed at the beginning or at the end of a sentence. It may also be divided within the sentence.
>   EXAMPLES: Deborah said, "There are sixty active members."
>   "Morton," asked Mrs. Sanchez, "have you read this magazine article?"

A. Add quotation marks and other punctuation where needed in the sentences below.

1. Uncle Dan, did you ever play football asked Tim.

2. Morris asked Why didn't you come in for an interview?

3. I have never said Laurie heard a story about a ghost.

4. Grandmother said Yuri thank you for the present.

5. When do we start on our trip to the mountains asked Stan.

6. Our guest said You don't know how happy I am to be in your house.

7. My sister said Kelly bought those beautiful baskets in Mexico.

8. I'm going to plant the spinach said Doris as soon as I get home.

> - Use an **apostrophe** in a contraction to show where a letter or letters have been taken out.
>   EXAMPLES: Amelia **didn't** answer the phone. **I've** found my wallet.
> - Use an apostrophe to form a possessive noun. Add -'s to most singular nouns. Add -' to most plural nouns. Add -'s to a few nouns that have irregular plurals.
>   EXAMPLES: A **child's** toy was in our yard. The **girls'** toys were in our yard. The **children's** toys were in our yard.

B. After each sentence below, write the word in which an apostrophe has been left out. Add the apostrophe where needed.

1. Many players uniforms are red. _____

2. That dog played with the babys shoe. _____

3. Julio isnt coming with us to the library. _____

4. Its very warm for a fall day. _____

5. The captains ship was one of the newest. _____

6. Marcia doesnt sing as well as my sister does. _____

7. Mens coats are sold in the new store. _____

■ Use a **colon** after the greeting in a business letter.
   EXAMPLES: Dear Sir: Dear Ms. Franklin:
■ Use a colon between the hour and the minute when writing time.
   EXAMPLES: 2:00 7:45 9:37
■ Use a colon to introduce a list.
   EXAMPLE: The suitcase contained these items: a toothbrush, a brush, a comb, and some clothing.

A. Add colons where needed in the sentences or phrases below.

1. The program begins at 8 3 0.

2. Dear Mrs. Sanchez

3. These are the students who must return library books Julia Turner, Carl Porter, Crystal Fletcher, and Asako Satoshi.

4. Beverly wakes up every morning at 6 1 5.

5. Dear Mr. Graham

■ Use a **hyphen** between the parts of some compound words.
   EXAMPLES: father-in-law   blue-black   well-known
              thirty-six   part-time   one-fourth
■ Use a hyphen to separate the syllables of a word that is carried over from one line to the next.
   EXAMPLE: After eating dinner, we watched a television show about tor-nadoes in the Midwest.

B. Add hyphens where needed in the sentences below.

1. A driving safety expert will visit our school to give a presen tation on seat belts.

2. There should be forty two people at the lecture.

3. I searched high and low, but I couldn't seem to find that new, yellow zip per I bought today.

4. My mother in law is coming from Florida.

5. In fifty eight years of driving, he has a nearly perfect record.

6. Ralph and Victor came late to the meeting, but Lora and Angela arrived ear ly and stayed late.

7. George could lift weights with ease, and Alberto was able to swim twenty one laps without stopping.

8. Our air conditioning unit broke on the hottest day of this summer.

9. Donna had to go inside to change her clothes because Scoot, her frisky pup py, got his muddy paws on her.

■ **Circle each letter that should be capitalized. Write the capital letter above it. Place punctuation marks where needed.**

1. have you seen miss nelson today____

2. elaine isnt major bill brandon your cousin____

3. mr. and mrs. john bell live at the mayflower apartments____

4. *alices adventures in wonderland* by lewis carroll is probably the fun

   niest book ive ever read____

5. how do people travel in the deserts of egypt____

6. *heidi* was written by johanna spyri____

7. im planning to spend christmas in florida with uncle will and aunt lee____

8. monticello is the beautiful home of thomas jefferson near

   charlottesville, virginia____

9. *jungle book* was written by rudyard kipling____

10. florida produces more oranges than any other state in the united states____

11. yes im sure she would replied sandra____

12. mrs. baldwin have you ever changed a flat tire____

13. *black beauty* is a famous story written by anna sewell____

14. mrs. perkins has written many interesting stories about the canadian

    alaskan and indian children____

15. isnt mount everest the highest mountain in the world____

16. have you ever crossed the rocky mountains____

17. how many miles does the st. lawrence river flow____

18. forty one students signed up for the field trip____

19. sometime i want to visit mexico city____

20. carol r. brink wrote a book about a boy in scotland____

21. the first monday in september is known as labor day____

22. i hope to get a part time job this summer____

A. Correct the stories below. Circle each letter that should be capitalized. Add missing periods, question marks, exclamation points, commas, quotation marks, colons, apostrophes, or hyphens where needed. Be sure to write the correct end punctuation on the blank after each sentence.

one of aesops fables is called "the fox and the crow____" it tells about a crow that stole a piece of cheese____ the crow landed on the branch of a tree put the cheese in her mouth and began to eat it____ but a fox was also interested in the cheese____ he sat under the branch and he thought about eating the cheese, too____

the fox said crow i compliment you on your size beauty and strength____ you would be the queen of all birds if you had a voice____

caw exclaimed the crow____

well the crow dropped the cheese____ the fox pounced on it carried it off a few feet and then turned around____

my friend said the fox you have every good quality except common sense____

_____

our neighbor denise baldwin likes to tell me funny stories____ one hot friday afternoon in august she told me about her trip to atlanta, georgia____ she was walking out of a store with some presents she had bought for pat her sister in law____ they were three joke gifts which included the following birthday candles that didnt blow out a silly hat and a mustache attached to some glasses____ denise accidentally bumped into another shopper____

im so sorry exclaimed denise____

are you hurt asked the other shopper____

no im not hurt said denise____ both shoppers had dropped their presents and they bent over to pick them up____

im denise baldwin she said as she picked up the presents____

my name is carol schwartz said the other shopper____

both shoppers said they were sorry again and thus went on their way____

denise gave her sister the presents when she returned to miami, florida____ pat had a puzzled look on her face when she unwrapped them____ the packages contained a rattle a bib and a baby bonnet____

oh gasped denise i must have picked up the wrong presents when i bumped into ms. schwartz____

whos ms. schwartz asked pat____

denise laughed and said i hope shes someone who likes joke gifts____

B. Rewrite the story below. Be sure to use capital letters and punctuation marks where they are needed.

sir walter scott one of the worlds greatest storytellers was born in edinburgh, scotland, on august 15, 1771____ walter had an illness just before he was two years old that left him lame for the rest of his life____ his par ents were worried so they sent him to his grandparents farm in sandy knowe____ they thought the country air would do him good____

walters parents were right____ he was quite healthy by the time he was six years old____ he was happy, too____ walter loved listening to his grandfather tell stories about scotland____ the stories stirred his imagination____ he began to read fairy tales travel books and history books____ it was these ear ly stories that laid the groundwork for Scotts later interest in writing stories____ his most famous book *Ivanhoe* has been read by people around the world____

Writing Sentences

- Every sentence has a base consisting of a simple subject and a simple predicate.
  EXAMPLE: Dolphins leap.
- Expand the meaning of a sentence by adding adjectives, adverbs, and prepositional phrases to the sentence base.
  EXAMPLE: **The sleek** dolphins **suddenly** leap **high into the air.**

A. Expand the meaning of each sentence base by adding adjectives, adverbs, and/or prepositional phrases. Write each expanded sentence.

1. (Dinner cooks.) _____

2. (Clown chuckled.) _____

3. (Car raced.) _____

4. (Dancer spun.) _____

5. (Panthers growled.) _____

6. (Leaves fall.) _____

7. (Bread baked.) _____

8. (Lake glistened.) _____

9. (Ship glides.) _____

B. Write five sentence bases. Then write an expanded sentence containing each sentence base.

1. _____

_____

2. _____

_____

3. _____

_____

4. _____

_____

5. _____

_____

> ■ A **topic sentence** is the sentence within a paragraph that states the main idea. It is often placed at the beginning of a paragraph.
>
> EXAMPLE:
>
> **The field trip to the state park was a great success.** First, the visitors learned a lot from their guide about the park. They learned that the forest was created by people, not by nature. To their surprise, they found out that the park had more than five hundred species of plants. Then they went on a hike and even spotted a falcon flying overhead. Finally, the visitors had a wonderful picnic lunch and headed back home.

A. Write a topic sentence for each paragraph below.

1. Some jewelry is made out of feathers, leather, shells, or wood. Other jewelry is crafted from gold, silver, brass, copper, or other metals. Gems and unusual stones are added for their beauty and value.

   Topic Sentence: _____

2. A pet goldfish needs clean water. A pump should be placed in the water to supply fresh air. The water temperature must be constant, and it must not go below 27°C (80°F). The goldfish should be fed flaked fish food or small insects.

   Topic Sentence: _____

3. When Jana crawls over to a kitchen cabinet, she whips the door open to see what's behind it. With a little help from Jana, the pots and pans are on the floor in no time. If she sees a bag of groceries, Jana has to investigate the contents. After she is tucked in bed for the night, this toddler loves to climb out of her crib and explore.

   Topic Sentence: _____

B. Write a topic sentence for each of the paragraph ideas below.

1. birthday parties _____

2. a great adventure _____

3. a great president _____

4. a favorite holiday _____

5. homework _____

6. video games _____

7. vacations _____

8. the Olympics _____

> ■ The idea expressed in a topic sentence can be developed with sentences containing **supporting details**. Details can include facts, examples, and reasons.

A. Read the topic sentence below. Then read the sentences that follow. Circle the seven sentences that contain details that support the topic sentence.

Topic Sentence: The Big Dipper Theme Park is a wonderful place to go for a fun-filled day.

1. The roller coaster is the most popular ride in the park.

2. The park was built in 1959.

3. You can test your pitching skills at the game booths.

4. You can win a stuffed animal at one of the pitching games.

5. Young children can enjoy a part of the park made especially for them.

6. We had sandwiches and potato salad for lunch.

7. The train ride is a pleasant way to relax and see the park.

8. However, the water rides are a great way to beat the heat.

9. What do you like to do during summer vacation?

10. The sky ride provides a grand tour of the park from high in the air.

B. Choose one of the topic sentences below. Write it on the first line. Then write five sentences that contain supporting details. The details can be facts, examples, or reasons.

1. Exercise is important for maintaining good health.

2. Being the oldest child in a family has its advantages.

3. The teen-age years are a time of change.

4. Videotapes have produced a breakthrough in the motion-picture industry.

_____

_____

_____

_____

_____

_____

_____

_____

- The **topic** of a paragraph is the subject of the paragraph.
- The **title** of a paragraph should be based on the topic.
- The **audience** is the person or persons who will read the paragraph.
  EXAMPLES: teachers, classmates, readers of the school newspaper, friends, family members

A. Suppose that you chose the topic <u>watching TV</u>. Underline the sentence that you would choose for the topic sentence.

1. Watching TV is one of the best ways to learn about things.

2. Watching TV is a waste of time.

3. The time children spend watching TV should be limited.

B. Think about the topic sentence you chose in Exercise A. Then underline the audience for whom you would like to write.

1. your classmates

2. your family members

3. readers of a newspaper

C. Write a paragraph beginning with the topic sentence you chose in Exercise A. Keep your audience in mind as you write. Be sure to write a title.

_____

_____

_____

_____

_____

_____

_____

_____

_____

_____

_____

> - **Note-taking** is an important step when writing a report.
> - You can find information for reports in encyclopedias, books, and magazines.
> - Before you begin, organize your research questions.
> - Write information accurately and in your own words.
> - Take more notes than you expect to need, so you won't have to go back to your sources a second time.

A. Underline a topic below that interests you.

1. a favorite hobby
2. the stars or planets
3. a historical figure
4. a species of animal
5. motion pictures

6. a favorite sport
7. a favorite food
8. fashion or costumes
9. gardening
10. airplanes

B. Gather some sources of information about your topic. Write the name of your topic on the first line below. For example, if you have chosen "a favorite food," you might write the name of that particular food. Then write notes about the topic on the remaining lines.

_____

- Organize your thoughts before writing by making an **outline.** An outline consists of the title of the topic, **main headings** for the main ideas, and **subheadings** for the supporting ideas.
- Main headings are listed after Roman numerals. Subheadings are listed after capital letters.

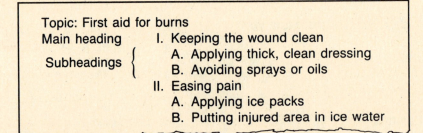

Topic: First aid for burns
Main heading   I. Keeping the wound clean
                  A. Applying thick, clean dressing
Subheadings {   B. Avoiding sprays or oils
           II. Easing pain
                 A. Applying ice packs
                 B. Putting injured area in ice water

- **Write an outline for the topic you chose in Exercise A on page 95. Use the sample outline as a guide.**

Topic: _____

   I. _____

      A. _____

      B. _____

  II. _____

      A. _____

      B. _____

  III. _____

      A. _____

      B. _____

  IV. _____

      A. _____

      B. _____

   V. _____

      A. _____

      B. _____

> ■ A **report** is a series of informative paragraphs covering a main topic. Each paragraph has a topic sentence and other sentences that contain supporting details. Begin with a paragraph that introduces the report, and end with a paragraph that concludes the report.

A. Read the paragraphs below.

Exploring the Mystery Planets: Uranus, Neptune, and Pluto

The planets Uranus, Neptune, and Pluto are difficult to study because of their distance from Earth. However, scientists are not completely without information about these planets. They know, for example, that Uranus is more than twice as far from Earth as Saturn is. They also know that Neptune is half again as far from Earth as Uranus. Both Saturn and Uranus are four times the size of Earth.

Scientists have explored the mysteries of Uranus. As Uranus orbits the sun every 84 years, it rolls around on its side. Although it is larger than Earth and orbits the sun more slowly, Uranus spins on its axis very rapidly. It completes a full rotation in 15 hours, 30 minutes. Five known satellites accompany Uranus, along with a system of nine dark rings that were discovered in 1977. The diameter of Uranus is 32,500 miles (52,200 kilometers), and the planet lies 1.78 billion miles (2.87 billion kilometers) from the sun. Because of this great distance, the temperature of Uranus is −360°F (−220°C), far too cold for any earth creature to survive.

Scientists have also explored the mysteries of Neptune. At a distance of 2.8 billion miles (4.5 billion kilometers) from the sun, Neptune appears through a telescope as a greenish-blue disc. Neptune is somewhat smaller than Uranus, having a diameter of about 30,000 miles. It is also very cold (−328°F, or −200°C). Two of Neptune's satellites have been named Nereid and Triton. In the summer of 1989, *Voyager 2* finally passed Neptune and, among other things, revealed that there are up to five rings around the planet.

It was 1930 before Pluto, the last planet in our solar system, was discovered. The "new" planet is 3.67 billion miles (6 billion kilometers) from the sun and takes 248 years to complete its orbit. In comparison, Earth takes only 365 days to complete a single orbit. While Pluto has not been measured exactly, scientists believe that it has a diameter of 1,600 miles (2,670 kilometers).

There are more interesting facts about Pluto. It also has a satellite, called Charon, which is five times closer to Pluto than our moon is to Earth. The yellowish color of Pluto indicates that it has very little atmosphere. Pluto's distance from the sun indicates that its climate is the coldest of the nine planets in our solar system.

Many mysteries remain concerning Uranus, Neptune, and Pluto, despite the fact that so much has been discovered. The questioning minds of the twenty-first century will continue our search for the secrets of space.

B. Circle the word or phrase that best completes each statement about this report.

1. Most of the report's supporting details are (facts, examples, reasons).

2. The writer of this report has included the (color, discoverer, diameter) of each of the three planets.

3. The writer does not discuss the relationship of the mystery planets to (Earth, Mars, the sun).

C. Underline the topic sentence in each paragraph.

■ **Revising** gives you a chance to rethink and review what you have written and to improve your writing. Revise by adding words and information, by taking out unneeded words and information, and by moving words, sentences, and paragraphs around.

■ **Proofreading** has to do with checking spelling, punctuation, grammar, and capitalization. Use proofreader's marks to show changes needed in your writing.

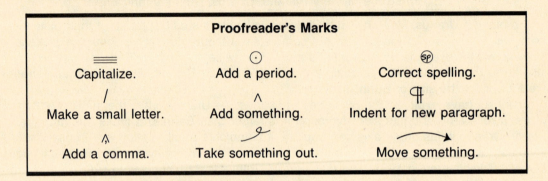

Proofreader's Marks

Capitalize.

Make a small letter.

Add a comma.

Add a period.

Add something.

Take something out.

Correct spelling.

Indent for new paragraph.

Move something.

A. Rewrite the paragraph below. Correct the errors by following the proofreader's marks.

yellowstone national park is the oldest and largest park national in the united states. It is located partly in northwestern wyoming, partly in southern montana, and partley in easturn idaho idaho. during the summur of 1988 large parts of park the were damaged by fire. A serious lack of rein was part of the reason the fire was sew severe. one fire threatened almost to destroy the park's famous lodge, which is constructed entirely of wood. fortunately, firefighters' efforts saved the lodge from desturction. today, the forests are slowly recovering from the fires.

_____

_____

_____

_____

_____

_____

B. Read the paragraphs below. Use proofreader's marks to revise and proofread the paragraphs. Then write your revised paragraphs below.

although yellowstons national park is the nation's largest national national park, other national parks are also well known yosemite national park in california has acres of Mountain Scenery and miles of hiking trails. Won of the world's largest biggest waterfalls can also be found in yosemite.

mammoth cave national park in kentucky features a huge underground cave the cave over has 212 miles of corridors it also have underground lakes rivers and waterfalls this cave system is estimated to be millions of years old

many pepul are surprized to learn that their are national parks in alaska and hawaii. mount McKinley the highest mountain in north america is located in denali national park in alaska. you can travel to hawaii and visit hawaii volcanoes national park this Park Has too active volcanoes rare plants and animals.

_____

_____

_____

_____

_____

_____

_____

_____

_____

_____

_____

_____

_____

_____

_____

_____

- A **business letter** has six parts.
  - The **heading** contains the address of the person writing and the date.
  - The **inside address** contains the name and address of the person to whom the letter is written.
  - The **greeting** tells to whom the letter is written. Use "Dear Sir or Madam" if you are unsure who will read the letter. Use a colon after the greeting in a business letter.
  - The **body** is the message of the letter. It should be brief, courteous, and to the point.
  - The **closing** is the ending that follows the body.
  - The **signature** is the name of the person who is writing the letter.
- When writing a business letter, remember the following:
  - Use business-size paper and envelopes.
  - Center your letter on the page, leaving at least a one-inch margin on each side.
  - Include specific information, such as quantities, sizes, numbers, brands, prices, manner of shipment, and amount of payment.
  - When you have finished, reread your letter. Rewrite it if you are not satisfied with any part of it.

A. Study this business letter. Then answer the questions below.

heading	572 Ironwood Avenue Orlando, FL 32887 April 4, 19____
inside address	Order Department Perfection Computer Company 9940 Main Street Brooklyn, NY 11227

greeting body	Dear Sir or Madam:
	    Please send me one copy of Making Friends With Your Computer. Enclosed is $7.95 to cover the cost of the book plus shipping and handling.
	    Thank you for your assistance.

closing	Sincerely yours,
signature	Chris Morrow Chris Morrow

1. Who wrote the letter? _____

2. What is the greeting? _____

3. Where is Perfection Computer Company located? _____

_____

4. When was the letter written? _____

Chris Morrow
572 Ironwood Avenue
Orlando, FL 32887

Order Department
Perfection Computer Company
9940 Main Street
Brooklyn, NY 11227

**B. Write a brief business letter asking for information about the Chicago Fire that you
can use in a report. Write to the Chicago Historical Society at 1600 Clark Street in
Chicago, Illinois. The zip code is 60610. Then circle the parts of the letter that would
appear on the envelope.**

A. **Write expanded sentences by adding adjectives, adverbs, and/or prepositional phrases to each sentence below.**

1. (Whistle blew.) _____

2. (Knights rode.) _____

3. (Fire trucks roared.) _____

B. **Write the six parts of a business letter in the order in which they appear in a letter.**

1. _____   body

2. _____   closing

3. _____   heading

4. _____   inside address

5. _____   greeting

6. _____   signature

C. **Write a possible topic sentence for each topic below.**

1. friendship _____

2. zoos _____

3. bicycles _____

D. **Circle the two sentences that contain details that support the topic sentence below.**

Topic Sentence: Rockets have many peacetime uses.

1. They are used to signal that a ship is in trouble.

2. High-performance rockets must have large nozzles.

3. Rockets carry cables across rivers for the construction of bridges.

E. **Find ten spelling, punctuation, and grammar errors in the paragraph below. Use the proofreader's marks on page 98 to mark the errors.**

Flying a kite can be fun, but it can also serve some practical purposes. For example, Benjamin franklin uses a kite in his experiments with electricity. In the early part of the twentieth century, box kites carring instruments measured wind speed temperature pressure and and humidity. they were also used to lift soldiers to hieghts where you could see the enemy. Today they serve as signals in air-see-rescue operations.

A. Write a report about the topic you chose on page 95. Use your outline and notes in writing the report. Be sure to write an interesting topic sentence for each paragraph and to use supporting details. Keep your audience in mind as you write. You may use the report on page 97 as a model. You might need to use your own paper.

B. Proofread and revise the report you wrote on page 103. Write your revised report below. You might need to use your own paper.

_____
_____
_____
_____
_____
_____
_____
_____
_____
_____
_____
_____
_____
_____
_____
_____
_____
_____
_____
_____
_____

> - A **dictionary** is a reference book that contains definitions of words and other information about their history and use.
> - **Entries** in a dictionary are listed in **alphabetical order.**
> - **Guide words** appear at the top of each dictionary page. Guide words show the first and last entry on the page.
>   EXAMPLE: The word <u>dog</u> would appear on a dictionary page with the guide words <u>dodge</u> / <u>doll</u>. The word <u>dull</u> would not.

A. Put a check in front of each word that would be listed on the dictionary page with the given guide words.

1. frozen / gather

_____ fruit

_____ grain

_____ furnish

_____ gate

_____ gallon

_____ former

_____ forgive

_____ fuzz

_____ galaxy

_____ future

2. money / muscle

_____ muddy

_____ moss

_____ motorcycle

_____ mustard

_____ moisten

_____ moose

_____ museum

_____ morning

_____ mortal

_____ modest

3. perfect / pin

_____ perfume

_____ pit

_____ pick

_____ photo

_____ pest

_____ plastic

_____ pillow

_____ pile

_____ pipe

_____ pizza

B. Number the words in each column in the order in which they would appear in a dictionary. Then write the words that could be the guide words for each column.

1. _____ / _____

_____ raccoon

_____ radar

_____ rabbit

_____ raisin

_____ react

_____ reflect

_____ rebel

_____ rainfall

_____ relay

_____ remind

_____ refuse

_____ ran

2. _____ / _____

_____ seize

_____ shellfish

_____ shrink

_____ signal

_____ silent

_____ scent

_____ shuffle

_____ shaft

_____ serpent

_____ seldom

_____ scope

_____ selfish

3. _____ / _____

_____ octopus

_____ olive

_____ of

_____ office

_____ old

_____ odor

_____ once

_____ oil

_____ odd

_____ onion

_____ occasion

_____ only

- A **syllable** is a part of a word that is pronounced at one time. Dictionary entry words are divided into syllables to show how they can be divided at the end of a writing line.
- A **hyphen (-)** is placed between syllables to separate them.
  EXAMPLE: man-a-ger
- If a word has a beginning or ending syllable of only one letter, do not divide it so that one letter stands alone.
  EXAMPLES: a-lone   sand-y

A. Write each word as a whole word.

1. ad-ver-tise _____

2. blun-der _____

3. par-a-dise _____

4. mis-chie-vous _____

5. con-crete _____

6. mi-cro-phone _____

7. in-ci-dent _____

8. val-ue _____

B. Find each word in a dictionary. Rewrite the word, placing a hyphen between each syllable.

1. bicycle _____

2. solution _____

3. category _____

4. punishment _____

5. behavior _____

6. quarterback _____

7. disappear _____

8. theory _____

9. wonderful _____

10. biology _____

11. sizzle _____

12. foreign _____

13. transparent _____

14. civilization _____

C. Write two ways in which each word may be divided at the end of a writing line.

1. mosquito _____mos-quito_____ _____mosqui-to_____

2. ambition _____ _____

3. boundary _____ _____

4. gingerbread _____ _____

5. geography _____ _____

6. leadership _____ _____

- Each dictionary entry word is followed by a respelling that shows how the word is **pronounced.**
- **Accent marks** (′) show which syllable or syllables are said with extra stress.
  EXAMPLE: hope-ful (hōp′ fəl)
- A **pronunciation key** (shown below) explains the other symbols used in the respellings.

A. Use the pronunciation key to answer the questions.

1. Which word contains an <u>a</u> that is pronounced the same

   as the <u>a</u> in <u>apple</u>? _____

2. How many words are given for the symbol ə? _____

3. Think of another word that contains the sound of ə.

   _____

4. What symbol represents the sound of the <u>wh</u> in <u>whether</u>? _____

5. What is the symbol for the pronunciation of <u>oo</u> in <u>boot</u>? _____

6. What is the symbol for the pronunciation of <u>th</u> in <u>themselves</u>? _____

> at; āpe; fär; câre; end; mē; it; īce; pîerce; hot; ōld; sông; fôrk; oil; out; up; ūse; rüle; pu̇ll; tûrn; chin; sing; shop; thin; <u>th</u>is; hw in white; zh in treasure. The symbol ə stands for the unstressed vowel sound in about, taken, pencil, lemon, and circus.

B. Use the pronunciation key to help you choose the correct word for each respelling. Underline the correct word.

1. (ə līv′)	olive	live	alive
2. (lōd)	load	lead	loud
3. (tro͞o)	threw	true	try
4. (thik)	thick	trick	tick
5. (fôl ən)	fallen	falling	fooling
6. (kāp)	cap	cop	cape
7. (īs)	is	ice	as
8. (<u>th</u>ā)	that	they	the
9. (sup′ ər)	super	support	supper
10. (lok′ ər)	locker	looker	lock
11. (hōm)	hum	hem	home
12. (fôt)	fought	fat	fit
13. (mīt)	mitt	meet	might
14. (fu̇l)	full	fuel	fool
15. (frēz)	froze	free	freeze
16. (let′ is)	lettuce	let's	less

- A dictionary lists the **definitions** of each entry word. Many words have more than one definition. In this case, the most commonly used definition is given first. Sometimes a definition is followed by a sentence showing a use of the entry word.
- A dictionary also gives the **part of speech** for each entry word. An abbreviation (shown below) stands for each part of speech. Some words might be used as more than one part of speech.

   EXAMPLE: **frost** (frôst) *n.* **1.** frozen moisture. *There was frost on all the leaves.* *-v.* **2.** to cover with frosting. *I'll frost the cake when it's cool.*

■ **Use the dictionary samples below to answer the questions.**

spec-i-fy (spes′ ə fī′) *v.* **1.** to say or tell in an exact way: *Please specify where we should meet you.* **2.** to designate as a specification: *The artist specified brown for the frame.*
spec-i-men (spes′ ə mən) *n.* **1.** a single person or thing that represents the group to which it belongs; example. **2.** a sample of something taken for medical purposes.

speck-le (spek′ əl) *n.* a small speck or mark. *-v.* to mark with speckles.
spec-tac-u-lar (spek tak′ yə lər) *adj.* relating to, or like a spectacle. *-n.* an elaborate show. — spec tac′ u lar ly, *adv.*

1. Which word can be used as either a noun

   or a verb? _____

2. Which word can be used only as a verb?

   _____

3. Which word can be used only as a noun?

   _____

n.	noun
pron.	pronoun
v.	verb
adj.	adjective
adv.	adverb
prep.	preposition

4. Which word can be used either as a noun or as an adjective? _____

5. Write a sentence using the first definition of spectacular. _____

   _____

6. Write a sentence using the first definition of specify. _____

   _____

7. Write a sentence using speckle as a verb. _____

   _____

8. Use the second definition of specimen in a sentence. _____

   _____

9. Which word shows an adverb form? _____

10. Which word shows two definitions used as a noun? _____

Dictionary: Word Origins

■ An **etymology** is the origin and development of a word. Many dictionary entries include etymologies. The etymology is usually enclosed in brackets [ ].
> EXAMPLE: **knit** [ME *knitten* < OE *cnyttan*, to knot]. The word *knit* comes from the Middle English word *knitten,* which came from the Old English word *cnyttan,* meaning "to tie in a knot."

■ **Use these dictionary entries to answer the questions.**

cam-pus (kam′ pəs) *n.* the grounds and buildings of a school or university. [Latin *campus,* meaning field, perhaps because most colleges used to be in the country.]

chaise longue (shāz lông′) *n.* a chair with a long seat which supports the sitter's outstretched legs. [French *chaise,* chair + *longue,* long.]

gar-de-nia (gär dēn′ yə) *n.* a fragrant yellow or white flower from an evergreen shrub or tree. [Modern Latin *Gardenia,* from Alexander *Garden,* 1730–1791, U.S. scientist who studied plants.]

pas-teur-ize (pas′ chə rīz) *v.* to heat food to a high temperature in order to destroy harmful bacteria. [From Louis *Pasteur,* inventor of the process.]

rent (rent) *n.* a regular payment for the use of property. [Old French *rente,* meaning taxes.]

ut-ter (ut′ ər) *v.* to express; make known; put forth. [From Middle English or Dutch, *utteren,* literally, out.]

wam-pum (wom′ pəm) *n.* small beads made from shells and used for money or jewelry. [Short for Algonquin *wampompeag,* meaning strings of money.]

1. Which word comes from an Algonquin word? _____

2. What does the Algonquin word mean? _____

3. Which word was formed from the name of an inventor? _____

4. Which word comes from French words? _____

5. What do the French words chaise and longue mean? _____

6. Which word was formed from the name of a scientist? _____

7. Which word is short for the word wampompeag? _____

8. Which words come from Latin words? _____

9. Which word comes from an English word? _____

10. What does the French word rente mean? _____

11. Which word comes from two languages? _____

12. What does the word utteren mean? _____

13. What does the Latin word campus mean? _____

14. Which word is the name of a flower? _____

15. Which word names a piece of furniture? _____

- A **title page** lists the name of a book and its author.
- A **copyright page** tells who published the book, where it was published, and when it was published.
- A **table of contents** lists the chapter or unit titles and the page numbers on which they begin. It is at the front of a book.
- An **index** gives a detailed list of the topics in a book and the page numbers on which each topic is found. It is in the back of a book.

A. Answer the questions below.

1. Where would you look to find when a book was published? _____

2. Where would you look to find the page number of a particular topic? _____

3. Where would you look to find the author's name? _____

4. Where would you look to find the titles of the chapters in a book? _____

B. Use your _Language Exercises_ book to answer the questions.

1. When was this book published? _____

2. Who is the publisher? _____

3. Where is the publishing company located? _____

4. On what page does Unit 6 begin? _____

5. On what page does the lesson on nouns begin? _____

6. What lesson begins on page 105? _____

7. What pages teach capitalization? _____

8. What page teaches indefinite pronouns? _____

9. What lesson begins on page 6? _____

10. What is the name of Unit 1? _____

11. What is the title of lesson 24? _____

12. On what page does Unit 2 begin? _____

13. What is the name of Unit 6? _____

14. On what page is the Unit 5 Review? _____

15. What is the title of lesson 38? _____

- Books on library shelves are arranged by **call numbers.** Each book is assigned a number from 000 to 999, according to its subject matter.
- The main subject groups for call numbers are as follows:

000–099 Reference	500–599 Science and Math
100–199 Philosophy	600–699 Technology
200–299 Religion	700–799 The Arts
300–399 Social Sciences	800–899 Literature
400–499 Languages	900–999 History and Geography

A. Write the call number group in which you would find each book.

1. *A Guide to Electronics in a New Age* _____

2. *A Traveler's Handbook of Everyday German* _____

3. *1991 World Almanac and Book of Facts* _____

4. *A History of the Roman Empire* _____

5. *The Modern Philosophers* _____

6. *Religions of the World* _____

7. *Solving Word Problems in Mathematics* _____

8. *Folktales of Norway* _____

9. *Painting with Watercolors* _____

10. *People in Society* _____

11. *Learn Spanish in Seven Days* _____

12. *Science Experiments for the Beginner* _____

13. *Technology in a New Century* _____

14. *Funny Poems for a Rainy Day* _____

15. *The Continent of Africa* _____

B. Write the titles of three of your favorite books. Write the call number group beside each title.

1. _____

2. _____

3. _____

■ The **card catalog** contains information cards on every book in the library. Some libraries are now computerized and have no card catalogs. But the information in the computer is filed in the same manner as the information in the card catalog.

■ Each book has three cards in the catalog. They are filed separately according to:
1. the author's last name
2. the subject of the book
3. the title of the book

A. Use the sample catalog card to answer the questions.

Author Card

Call number —— 597.31 S252

Sattler, Joan Marie —— Author

Title —— Sharks : the super fish ; illustrated by

Jean Day Sallinger. — New York : Lothrop, —— Publisher

Date published —— © 1986. —— Place published

Number of pages —— 96 p. : illus. —— Illustrated

1. What is the author's name? _____

2. What is the title of the book? _____

3. How many pages does the book have? _____

4. What is the call number of the book? _____

5. When was the book published? _____

6. What subject might this book be filed under? _____

B. Write author, title, or subject to tell which card you would look for to locate the book or books.

1. books about national parks in the United States _____

2. *The Adventures of Huckleberry Finn* _____

3. a novel by Sylvia Cassidy _____

4. books about Helen Keller _____

5. a book of poems by Vachel Lindsay _____

6. *Children's Verse in America* _____

- An **encyclopedia** is a reference book that contains articles on many different subjects. The articles are arranged alphabetically in volumes. Each volume is marked to show which articles are inside.
- Guide words are used to show the first topic on each page.
- At the end of most articles there is a listing of cross-references to related topics for the reader to investigate.

■ **Read each sample encyclopedia entry below. Then refer to each to answer the questions that follow.**

BIRDSEYE, Clarence (1886–1956), was an American food expert and inventor. Birdseye was born in Brooklyn, N.Y., and educated at Amherst College. He is best known for developing methods of preserving foods and for marketing quick-frozen foods. He also worked on lighting technology, wood-pulping methods, and heating processes. *See also* FOOD PROCESSING.

1. Whom is the article about? _____

2. When did he live? _____

3. Where did he go to college? _____

4. What is he best known for? _____

5. What else did he work on? _____

6. What other article in the encyclopedia is related to the subject? _____

FOOD PROCESSING is a process by which food is protected from spoiling for future use. Preserved food should look, taste, and feel like the original food. Many methods are used today to preserve food.
Canning In this process, food is sterilized through heat treatments and sealed in airtight containers. Canned food stored in the cold of Antarctica was preserved for 50 years. This would not be true of canned food stored in hot climates.
Freezing The freezing process was not widely used until the late 19th century. Freezing does not kill all types of bacteria, and care must be taken that foods are not thawed and refrozen. Freezing has the advantage of keeping food looking more like the fresh product than canning does.

7. Why do you think this cross-reference is included in the article about Birdseye?

_____

_____

8. Does the above cross-reference mention Clarence Birdseye? _____

When looking for an article in the encyclopedia:
- Always look up the last name of a person.
  - EXAMPLE: To find an article on Helen Keller, look under Keller.
- Look up the first word in the name of a city, state, or country.
  - EXAMPLE: To find an article on Puerto Rico, look under Puerto.
- Look up the most specific word in the name of a geographical location.
  - EXAMPLE: To find an article on Lake Erie, look under Erie.
- Look up the most significant word in the name of a general topic.
  - EXAMPLE: To find an article on neon lamps, look under neon.

A. The example below shows how the volumes of a particular encyclopedia are marked to indicate the alphabetical range of the articles they cover. Write the number of the volume in which you would find each article.

A	B	C–CH	CI–CZ	D	E	F	G	H	I–J	K	L
1	2	3	4	5	6	7	8	9	10	11	12

M	N	O	P	Q–R	S–SH	SI–SZ	T	U–V	W–X–Y–Z
13	14	15	16	17	18	19	20	21	22

1. camping _____

2. North Dakota _____

3. Jonathan Swift _____

4. the Beatles _____

5. Los Angeles _____

6. John F. Kennedy _____

7. Mount Rushmore _____

8. sand flea _____

9. New Guinea _____

10. Babe Ruth _____

11. Caspian Sea _____

12. Smith College _____

13. Victor Hugo _____

14. elementary school ____

15. Lake Ontario _____

B. Look up the following articles in an encyclopedia. Write a cross-reference for each article.

1. bee _____

2. X-ray _____

3. atom _____

4. music _____

5. Georgia _____

6. space travel _____

7. Susan B. Anthony _____

8. cartoon _____

C. Choose a person who interests you, and find the entry for that person in an encyclopedia. Then answer the questions below.

1. Who is the person you've chosen? _____

2. When did this person live? _____

3. What made this person famous? _____

4. What encyclopedia did you use? _____

Choosing Reference Sources

> - Use a **dictionary** to find the definitions and pronunciations of words, suggestions for word usage, and etymologies.
> - Use an **encyclopedia** to find articles about many different people, places, and other subjects. Also use an encyclopedia to find references to related topics.
> - Use an **atlas** to find maps and other information about geographical locations.

■ **Write encyclopedia, dictionary, or atlas to show which source you would use to find the following information. Some topics might be found in more than one source.**

1. the pronunciation of the word <u>measure</u> _____

2. the location of Yellowstone National Park _____

3. the care and feeding of a dog _____

4. the distance between Rome and Naples _____

5. jewelry throughout the ages _____

6. planning a vegetable garden _____

7. the meaning of the word <u>federal</u> _____

8. the etymology of the word <u>consider</u> _____

9. the early life of Abraham Lincoln _____

10. the states through which the Mississippi River flows _____

11. how volcanoes form _____

12. a definition of the word <u>ape</u> _____

13. the rivers and mountains of Canada _____

14. how paper is made _____

15. the location of the border between China and the U.S.S.R. _____

16. the history of kite making _____

17. the pronunciation of the word <u>particular</u> _____

18. the names of lakes in Northern California _____

19. the meanings of the homographs of <u>bow</u> _____

20. methods of scoring in football _____

■ **Use the dictionary samples to answer the questions below.**

tux-e-do (tuk sē′ dō) *n.* a man's formal suit, usually black, having a jacket with satin lapels and trousers with a stripe of satin along the outer side of each leg. [From *Tuxedo Park, New York*, an exclusive community where this suit was popular during the nineteenth century.]
tweed (twēd) *n.* **1.** a woolen fabric, woven with fibers of two or more colors. **2. tweeds.** clothing made of tweed.

twin (twin) *n.* **1.** one of two offspring born at the same birth. **2.** either of two people, animals, or things that are very much or exactly alike. *-adj.* **1.** being one of two born as twins. **2.** being one of two things that are very much or exactly alike: *The fort had twin towers. -v.* to give birth to twins.
twin-kle (twing′ kəl) *v.* to gleam or flash with light. *The lights twinkle at night. -n.* a flicker or sparkle of light.

1. What part of speech is <u>tweed</u>? _____ <u>tuxedo</u>? _____

2. How many definitions are given for <u>tuxedo</u>? _____

3. How many definitions are given for the noun <u>twin</u>? _____

4. Which word can be used as an adjective? _____

5. Which word comes from the name of a place in New York? _____

6. How many syllables are there in <u>tuxedo</u>? _____

   in <u>tweed</u>? _____   in <u>twinkle</u>? _____

7. Underline the pair of words that could be guide words for the dictionary entries above.

   a. turtle / twill   **c.** tusk / twirl

   b. twang / twist   **d.** Tuscan / twig

8. Which words can be used as both a noun and a verb? _____

9. Which entry includes an etymology? _____

10. Which words are used in example sentences? _____

11. Write one sentence using the second adjective definition of <u>twin</u>. _____

    _____

12. Write the correct word for each respelling.

    a. (twing′ kəl) _____   **b.** (tuk sē′ dō) _____

13. Which words can be used as verbs? _____

14. Which word has the most definitions? _____

15. Write one sentence using the second definition of <u>tweed</u>. _____

    _____

16. Write one sentence using <u>twinkle</u> as a noun. _____

    _____

A. Use a textbook with an index to answer the questions.

1. Copy the title from the title page. _____

2. Write the name(s) of the author(s). _____

3. What is the name of the publisher? _____

4. Name two other pieces of information that you can find on the copyright page. _____

_____

5. How many units or chapters are listed in the table of contents? _____

6. In what part of the book can you find the index? _____

7. Choose a topic from the book that you have studied. Use the index to find the page numbers where

this topic can be located. Write the page numbers. _____

8. Name a chapter or unit in which this topic appears. _____

B. Use the sample catalog card to answer the questions.

	CHINA
915.1	
M978	Murphy, Joseph D.
	Adventures beyond the clouds: how we climbed
	China's mountains. —
	Minneapolis, MN: Dalton Press, ©1986
	135 p.: col. illus.

1. What kind of catalog card is this? _____

   a. title card   **b.** subject card   **c.** author card

2. Who is the author of this book? _____

3. What is the title? _____

4. Who is the publisher? _____

5. Is the book illustrated? _____

6. What is the call number? _____

7. How many pages are there? _____

8. When was the book published? _____

C. Use an encyclopedia to complete the following exercises.

1. What is the name of the encyclopedia you are using?

_____

2. List the volume number in which you would find each topic in your encyclopedia.

_____ **a.** Margaret Thatcher   _____ **h.** South Carolina

_____ **b.** North Carolina   _____ **i.** post office

_____ **c.** Mount Holly   _____ **j.** Benjamin Franklin

_____ **d.** Niagara Falls   _____ **k.** country music

_____ **e.** Mahatma Gandhi   _____ **l.** Missouri River

_____ **f.** New Zealand   _____ **m.** Indian Ocean

_____ **g.** Olympic Games   _____ **n.** Walt Disney

3. Look up each subject in your encyclopedia. Write a cross-reference for each subject.

a. Paiute Indians _____

b. Lincoln Memorial _____

c. canoe racing _____

d. pirate _____

e. library _____

f. Robert R. Livingston _____

4. Choose a sport that interests you, and find the entry for that sport in an encyclopedia. Then write a paragraph that tells how, when, and where the sport began.

_____

_____

_____

_____

_____

_____

_____

_____

_____

Synonyms, Antonyms, Homonyms, and Homographs ▪ On the line bei
words, write <u>S</u> if they are synonyms, <u>A</u> if they are antonyms, <u>H</u> if they are ho
and <u>HG</u> if they are homographs.

1. _____ far, close

2. _____ discover, find

3. _____ great, grate

4. _____ shut, closed

5. _____ mistake, error

6. _____ jagged, smooth

7. _____ ring, ring

8. _____ here, hear

9. _____ call, shout

10. _____ herd, heard

11. _____ plane, plain

12. _____ tall, short

13. _____

14. _____ bea

15. _____ together,

16. _____ sun, son

17. _____ honest, truthful

18. _____ jar, jar

Prefixes and Suffixes ▪ Add a prefix or suffix to the underlined word in each sentence to form a new word that makes sense in the sentence. Write the new word in the blank.

1. My parents always said that anything is <u>possible</u> if you always tell yourself

   that nothing is _____.

2. That man's business is a <u>success</u>, and he thanks his employees for making the past year

   the most _____ in the company's history.

3. The baseball coach tells us we'll win more games if we never let ourselves <u>tire</u>

   and are _____ in our practice.

4. It took many hours to <u>write</u> and then _____ the term paper
   to get it ready to hand in.

5. None of us were <u>certain</u> why we felt so _____ about which road
   to take.

Contractions and Compound Words ▪ Write the two words that make up the contraction in each sentence. Then underline the compound word in each sentence, and draw a line between the two words that make up each compound word.

1. _____ _____ "Where's the airplane museum?" asked Anne.

2. _____ _____ "I think it's downtown," said Steve.

3. _____ _____ "Isn't that the headquarters of the parachute club?"
   asked Tim.

4. _____ _____ "Yes, they're in the same high-rise," said Steve.

5. _____ _____ "Is that the building where you can't see the rooftop?"
   asked Anne.

rite **D** for declarative, **IN** for interrogative,
uate each sentence correctly.

5. _____ Where's the best spot____

6. _____ I feel lucky____

7. _____ Look at that splash____

8. _____ I think it's a trout____

ie between the complete subject and the complete
derline the simple subject once and the simple

pred

1. Bicycling i_____ all ages can enjoy.

2. Cyclists can learn ha_____ and traffic rules.

3. Many cyclists wear special biking clothes and shoes.

4. A helmet is an important safety item.

5. Experts recommend that cyclists always stay in control of their bikes.

6. City riders should learn how to ride in traffic.

Compound Sentences ▪ Combine each pair of sentences below to form a compound sentence.

1. Carlos likes to ride his bike in the park. Anita prefers to ride to school.

_____

2. A bicycle safety course is offered after school. The class is for ten people.

_____

3. A bike maintenance course will be held in the fall. Students will learn how to
repair and maintain their bikes.

_____

**Correcting Run-on Sentences and Expanding Sentences ▪ Correct the run-on
sentences. Then expand each new sentence by adding details.**

1. The cyclists rode, the rider in front led.

a. _____

b. _____

2. Judges held stopwatches, riders crossed the finish line.

a. _____

b. _____

Grammar and Usage ■ **Fill in the blanks by supplying the word or words specified in parentheses.**

Trees are important for _____ products and their benefits to the
(possessive pronoun)

environment. Wood _____ one of the main building supplies in the
(present tense of <u>be</u>)

world and an important fuel. Paper and paper products _____ from
(helping verb and verb)

wood pulp. Trees also _____ _____ nuts
(present tense verb)   (adjective)

and fruits for both _____ and humans.
(common noun)

One way _____ help the environment is by releasing oxygen
(plural of <u>tree</u>)

_____ the air. For instance, if a tree has _____
(preposition)   (past participle of <u>take</u>)

in sunlight and carbon dioxide, it _____ oxygen. Tree roots help
(future tense of <u>release</u>)

control erosion and flooding. Trees have always _____ homes
(past participle of <u>give</u>)

_____ shelter for _____ animals.
(conjunction)   (adjective)

Raccoons, _____, and other animals _____
(common noun)   (present tense verb)

their homes _____ trees.
(preposition)

_____ trees have lived and _____ for
(adjective)   (past participle of <u>grow</u>)

thousands of years and are hundreds of feet tall. The redwoods in California are some of the

_____ trees in the world. The tallest tree is 364 feet tall and lives
(superlative adjective)

_____ Humboldt National Forest. The _____
(preposition)   (superlative adjective)

living tree is a bristlecone pine in Nevada that is _____ 4,600 years old.
(adverb)

Capitalization and End Punctuation ▪ Circle each letter that should be capitalized.
Write the capital letter above it. Add correct end punctuation to each sentence.

1. did you know there was an eclipse of the moon in august____

2. people all over the united states and the world could see it____

3. professor almorez brought a group of students to look-out mountain to observe the eclipse____

4. his class compared notes with a class from petersville junior high in st. louis, missouri____

5. he recommended that both classes read *lunar and solar eclipses* by dr. joanne crowell____

6. the students were asked to finish their reading for tuesday____

7. professor almorez said, "have questions ready to ask me on monday____"

8. one of the students reminded prof. almorez that monday was memorial day____

9. "oh, that's right," said the professor____ "take an extra day on your assignments____"

10. "remember to look for the big dipper this weekend," added the professor____

Punctuation and Capitalization ▪ Circle each letter that should be capitalized below.
Add commas, quotation marks, apostrophes, periods, colons, and hyphens where needed.

122 e. park street
denver, co 81442
october 10, 1990

mr. marshall chase
3910 prairie avenue
lowell, ma 01740

Dear mr. chase

thank you very much for your interest in my star gazing book a guide to the stars____ i published it in september through a well known astrology publisher the skys the limit press____ according to my publisher, books will be available at bookstores this month____

i have the answer to your question on how I do my research____ i have a very powerful telescope that i use every day____ i do most of my work at night between 1015 P.M. and 130 A.M.____ i find those to be the darkest hours out here in colorado____ finally, i have a piece of advice for budding astronomers____ always keep a journal of the stars you see each night and try to memorize their location____ i always say to my students the skys the limit____ good luck star gazing____

Sincerely,
professor liz nelson

Topic Sentences ▪ Write a topic sentence for the paragraph below. Name a possible audience for the paragraph.

All children and adults should learn basic first aid. Courses are offered through schools and community groups. You never know when you'll need to clean a wound or use a more difficult technique during an emergency. By knowing first aid, you'll always be prepared.

Topic Sentence: _____

Audience: _____

Revising and Proofreading ▪ Rewrite the paragraph below. Correct the errors by following the proofreader's marks.

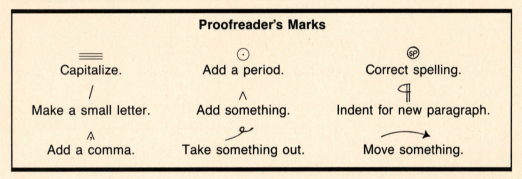

Proofreader's Marks		
Capitalize.	Add a period.	Correct spelling.
Make a small letter.	Add something.	Indent for new paragraph.
Add a comma.	Take something out.	Move something.

¶ did you know that roughly three-quarters of the earth's fresh water is held not in rivers and lakes?

the water is held in glaciers lage sheets of ice that form in high altitudes and polar regions such

as antarctica and Greenland their are between 70,000 and 200,000 glaicers in the world.

¶ as temperatures warm glaciers melt a little and move at a wrate that can't bee seen as they

move they sometimes freize and add to their mass before moving on they actually reshape

the land they pass ovver.

_____

_____

_____

_____

_____

_____

_____

_____

_____

Composition

Using the Dictionary ▪ Use the dictionary samples to answer the questions.

firm (furm) *adj.* **1.** unyielding to pressure; steady **2.** unchanging, established. *The company had a firm customer base.* **3.** tough and hard. *The apple had a firm skin.* *-n.* a business partnership. [Old French *ferme*, meaning strong]

fleet (flēt) *n.* **1.** a group of battle or warships under unified command. **2.** a group operating or working (such as ships, cars, or planes) under unified command. *The fleet of trucks reported to their dispatcher at 5:00 a.m.* [Old English *fleot*, meaning a ship or ships.]

1. Circle the letter of the guide words for the above entries.

    a. flag / fleece   **b.** float / flood   **c.** fire / flight

2. How many definitions are listed for firm? _____ fleet? _____

3. Write one sentence using the third definition of firm.

_____

4. Write a sentence using firm as a noun. _____

_____

5. What part of speech is fleet? _____

6. How many syllables do fleet and firm have? _____

7. Write the respelling of fleet. _____ firm. _____

8. Which word came from the Old French word ferme? _____

Reference Sources ▪ Write encyclopedia, dictionary, or atlas to tell where you would find the following information.

1. the height of Mt. Everest _____

2. the definition of the word astronomy _____

3. the birthdate of George Washington _____

4. the longest river in Germany _____

5. the location of the border between Canada and the United States _____

6. how earthquakes develop _____

7. a synonym for the word carry _____

8. the inventions of Marie Curie _____

9. the etymology of the word pencil _____

st part of the Pacific Ocean _____

23

_____